LinkedIn Revealed:

The Professional Network Your Career Can't Afford To Ignore

Looking to advance your career, but feel stuck in your current position? Looking to switch your career path, but overwhelmed in your search?

Discover how to build a thriving professional network by tapping into the most influential social network for career advancement – LinkedIn.

By

Jonathan Kidder (Author)
&
Brian Patrick (Co-Author & Editor)

LinkedIn Revealed:

The Professional Network Your Career Can't Afford To Ignore

GrassRoot Books
BR Industries LLC
www.grassrootbooks.com

Editors' Note:

Attention: Your Career Needs You!

Industries are disappearing, companies are gutting their bureaucratic composition, and individuals are responsible of taking charge of their career and financial success more than any other time in history.

Change is inevitable; change is also inevitably empowering. The days are over where pension plans were commonplace and gold watches were handed out to those retiring from their 40-year tenure with the same company. Gen-Y now gets blamed for not their "non-loyal" ways as they continue to change jobs like they change their clothes. However, the new workforce is facing immense change. The current day career arena is completely unpredictable and employees are simply attempting to adapt to constant change.

Now, more than ever, are we in control of our career plight. Many skillsets once in demand are no longer needed, and many in-demand skills aren't being formally taught at traditional institutions. There's massive oversupply of talent in some fields, whereas newer fields such as computer programming are desperately seeking talent.

With industries, companies, and universities playing catch up to the evolving needs of businesses and the wants of consumers, it's becoming essential that individuals invest in themselves by building and curating a valuable professional network.

Those in traditional publishing didn't just wave the white flag after the advent of the eBook; they adapted to industry demands, tapped into their network for support, and became eBook publishers. Those working for the Yellowpages didn't pack up their belongings when online search engines came to town. They quickly steered their career development to learn these new platforms and became pioneers of online advertisement.

How Can You Make Sure Your Career Stays Relevant?

Networking with intent. This has always been the case, except now you can network online. Not only can you connect with your "real world" network online, but you can also expand and empower your network with incredible efficiency.

LinkedIn is the foremost online social network for career professionals. The hundreds of millions of users on LinkedIn did not join to share pictures of their puppies or rant about their daily commute. LinkedIn is the ultimate platform in securing one's connectivity to their industry and profession.

It's time to take charge of your career, and that starts with developing your professional network online with the most rewarding professional platform available. This book provides all of the advice needed to leverage LinkedIn, helping you architect a blazing career path, and configure a network that will continue to support your career ambitions well into the future.

While there is no substitute for in-person networking, the advent of Web 2.0 helps one capture and foster those in-person interactions and relationships. Furthermore, with the widespread popularity of Web 2.0 and LinkedIn specifically, one can now supplement in-person networking in a much more efficient manner.

We've assembled this book for those 90% of LinkedIn users who've yet to unleash the true power behind this professional network. While every reader will have their own intentions for using LinkedIn, we will cover all of the essential aspects that can be leveraged without a premium subscription. There will be certain instruction for those with a specific goal in mind, such as finding a job or landing a new client, but all readers will learn how to assemble an extremely rewarding network that will make any career maneuver a seamless one.

It's Time To Catapult Your Career!

Jonathan Kidder & Brian Patrick

Table Of Contents

About The Authors

Jonathan Kidder - is a strategic marketing professional and talent community manager for one of the largest privately held staffing companies in the world. He helps connect recruiters with the most talented professionals, and on the flipside, helps such talented candidates establish their position in the job market. In short, he simplifies the hiring process for his company by bringing in the most talented candidates. Having worked with both recruiters and career professionals, Jonathan has become a LinkedIn expert, finding it to be the most effective channel for professionals to advance their professional careers through networking.

He's received acknowledgement from LinkedIn's Senior Vice President of Products & User Experience, Deep Nishar, as being a top 1% of the Most Viewed LinkedIn profiles for 2012. This is awarded to the top users of LinkedIn whom have maximized engagement on the network.

Brian Patrick - is a digital marketing professional who has worked both in the field of recruiting and in within the digital advertising arena. Specifically, he has specialized in the area of Search Engine Optimization, better known as SEO. This is the practice of optimizing digital assets such as websites, profiles, and other online properties in order to receive higher visibility.

Applying this knowledge in his businesses, he has helped clients' websites generate more traffic and has also helped career professionals become more visible within LinkedIn.

More than 200 million people have created an account on LinkedIn; for 90% of these users, that's all they've done. Creating a profile on LinkedIn is simple. Getting noticed on a platform this large is the hard part and that is why Brian and Jonathan have put together this book.

How To Use This Book To Catapult Your Career

The content of this book is positioned in specific order so those looking to take action can read and apply instruction from front to back cover. The majority of the book covers essential LinkedIn strategies for building your profile and ramping up networking efforts. Additional instruction has been included to help those looking for specific guidance, especially in relation to career change and how to leverage LinkedIn to generate business leads.

First, we will address LinkedIn basics. This includes navigating the platform, understanding the specific terminology, and setting proper expectations. Furthermore, we will breakdown all of the settings controlling your networking experience. Adjusting these settings must be taken seriously as even the smallest changes can be very impactful to your success on LinkedIn. With the basics addressed, we will walk through the process of creating an optimized profile. Not until you've optimized your profile can you begin taking full advantage of all the networking features made available.

At this point, we will look at the most powerful networking features on LinkedIn and how to best utilize them. This section on networking will feature the most important instruction of the book. Adopting successful networking skills will result in the development of a highly valuable professional network, one that will continuously support and push your career forward.

The information and practical application provided in these chapters will be more than adequate in helping you become a highly proficient LinkedIn user. At this point, you will be better versed on LinkedIn than 90-95% of users.

Applying the various profile optimizations and networking strategies, your efforts will help you quickly surpass other users' traction and results on the platform. You will be able to withdraw a lot more value from your network because you will have taken the time to build and engage a network full of professionals relevant to your career goals. Additionally, you will understand how to utilize all of the features, many of which are lesser known, to help you accomplish specific networking tasks.

Lastly, we will look at supplemental features and strategies not yet mentioned. This section will act more as a reference point in helping those users with particular networking goals. While building a highly targeted network is mandatory for all users looking to master engagement on LinkedIn, this instruction will help those currently looking for a career change and those looking to generate leads for business.

At the very end, several resources that didn't find their way into the text are listed, as well the resources mentioned throughout the book.

Part One: What Is LinkedIn And Why Your Career Can't Afford To Ignore It

In the past decade, the nature of the job search has undergone extreme change. Job listings in newspapers have evolved to company career websites, and these postings have lead to the creation of massive online job boards such as Monster.com. With job searching and the hiring process becoming a more navigable experience, corporations now have endless options for finding and attracting talented candidates.

Today, once a company places a new job listing on their own career website, it instantly gets reposted to career aggregation websites such as Monster.com or Indeed.com. Job seekers, with accounts on these websites, are then notified via email of these new openings. Furthermore, employees can now share job openings by way of their social networks with ease; many in hopes that a friend may be interested, as most companies offer an employee referral bonus.

Although there may be less job openings due to the current state of the economy, finding opportunities has become a much easier task with liberation of the job search processes. Not only are jobs easier to find, they are now easier to apply to; instant resume and application submissions are made possible with career websites and online job boards. The combination of a less burdensome application process and fewer opportunities has resulted in a battle for attention. Candidates can easily display their interest for a job opening, yet most are finding it nearly impossible to capture the interest of hiring managers.

From a recruiters' standpoint, it has become extremely difficult to wade through the increasing amount of applications to find the top talent. We recruiters must now sift through hundreds and even thousands of applications for individual job postings; on the flipside, candidates must really standout for us to take notice.

Recruiters are constantly looking for new ways to quickly evaluate candidates. With the advent of social media, privacy is now a thing of the past. Candidates can no longer hide behind their resume or cover letter and expect great results. Transparency on all fronts is now the norm. Employers, armed with Google, now have the ability to scrutinize every candidate applying for their positions.

This transparency is neither good nor bad. Unless someone is out to slander your name, you have great control of what others can discover about you online. Computer programmers can showcase all of the software they've built. Photographers can upload their portfolio to photo sharing websites and build their own photography website. If you take care in assembling your online presence, transparency can become a key advantage in garnering positive attention.

Recruiters are constantly squeezed for time; there are always more job openings that need attention and never enough time to review all of the applicants. To combat the piles of resumes in their inboxes, recruiters now rely on tools to streamline their work.

Prepared with just a LinkedIn subscription and a few advanced search strategies, we can evaluate candidates quicker than ever. We can filter applicants by almost any criteria, including experience, skillsets, location, previous employers, and so on and so forth. Of the thousands that apply for a job posting, any competent recruiter paired with a LinkedIn account can narrow the field down to a few qualified applicants in a matter of minutes.

Regardless of whether you are a job seeker or not, your professional and personal information is out there for all to see. Those that are proactive in dictating what information about them is made available will benefit; those that neglect this new transparency will end up in a worse off position.

There may be times where information about you becomes available online in which you have no control over. However, your online presence is usually directly correlated to your offline presence. If you are an industry thought leader that speaks at conferences, your keynote addresses are probably available on YouTube. If you are a community activist, your efforts may be documented on various local websites and news sources. While you may not have direct control of what is made available, you do have indirect control through what you activities you participate in.

Unless you are running for president, the photo of you on Facebook drinking a beer at a holiday party will not be held against you. People understand that Facebook is the social network for personal use and engage with the network as such. Most companies actually prefer to speak with well-rounded candidates that participate in extracurricular activities, granted drinking beer isn't your only hobby.

However, LinkedIn has its own etiquette and it's vital that users approach this platform with expectations of how their online presence can be enhanced.
LinkedIn, also known as the "Professional Network" has become the de facto network for career advancement. Users of LinkedIn don't expect, nor will tolerate, unprofessional engagement.

LinkedIn provides you the opportunity to take the reins of your professional persona. Just as socialites boast an incredibly vast network on Facebook, those professionals interested in career development will leverage LinkedIn to build a thriving network.

What Is LinkedIn?

In the time it takes you to read this sentence, at least 10 people have created a profile on LinkedIn. At a rate of 2 new members per second, this professional network is growing at a pace only matched by few other member-based websites.

LinkedIn is the world's largest professional network on the Internet. It is now publicly traded on the New York Stock Exchange under the stock symbol LNKD. Founded by former PayPal Board Member, Reid Hoffman, LinkedIn's membership now boasts over 200 million members, of which almost half are based in the U.S.

Reid Hoffman built this "social network" in a very strategic manner. From the very beginning, Hoffman positioned LinkedIn as the network for career driven individuals. No other professional network comes close in size or influence.

With the company's mission clearly defined, LinkedIn only attracts those individuals looking to participate in a professional environment. The result: LinkedIn is commonly noted for it's affluent membership, with the average member's household income exceeding $100,000.

Additionally, LinkedIn reports that 93% of its users are more likely to be college graduates than the average adult online. Results from a recent poll show that more than 2/3's of all members join LinkedIn with the intent of networking with other professionals, fostering their professional identity, and keeping up with industry news.
(http://marketing.LinkedIn.com/audience)

Combine a wealthy, educated membership with an explicit intent on professional development and you have one incredibly powerful network. While some members flock to LinkedIn with a certain purpose, such as finding a job, many users end up getting lost and frustrated by the overwhelming options and possibilities. For those less tech savvy individuals and social media newcomers, LinkedIn may seem too challenging. Even recent college graduates and Gen-Y users, who make up a sizable portion of the overall membership, struggle with LinkedIn because it requires a completely different approach than the social networks they are accustomed to. That is why we must set expectations for using this platform. It's not difficult to navigate LinkedIn, but many users will abandon ship because they had the wrong expectations, or none, which is worse.

Setting & Realizing Expectations

Many individuals do join LinkedIn with certain intent. This intent may be to network, job search, or research a new career path. Regardless of intent, a lot of these users end up neglecting their accounts for one reason or another and this can be extremely to one's online presence.

Unlike other social media sites or web applications, a barren and unattended LinkedIn account can be very costly to your career. Just by joining LinkedIn, you are announcing to the professional world that you are present and ready to network. Aside from the 10% of LinkedIn users that properly leverage the network to their advantage, the remaining 90% either fall into one of the following two categories.

The first group of users is those who neglect their account. This includes not filling out their profile completely, not uploading a professional photo, and ignoring many of the features that could lead to career advancement. These users are either lost and need help in getting familiar with the platform, or their expectations were misinformed. They assume that just by signing up for an account, opportunities would be awaiting their arrival.

The second group of users encompasses those that don't neglect their LinkedIn account, but rather use the platform incorrectly to achieve their goals. These users have correct expectations, whether it is networking, seeking job opportunities, or career research. However, they struggle to identify and execute the crucial strategies in achieving such expectations. The majority of these users have incorrectly set up their profile. They have included past job information, but leave out skillsets used for these jobs. They include a profile picture, but it's outdated and unprofessional. They write an inspiring, attention-grabbing headline, but leave out important keywords that other professionals are most likely searching for.

16

Not surprisingly, the majority of people not benefitting from LinkedIn happen to fall within the second group. Because LinkedIn boasts and attracts such a driven demographic, most people on LinkedIn are active and use the platform with great intention. Unfortunately, only few people have taken the time to learn proper LinkedIn "etiquette" and leverage it to accomplish their goals.

What You Can Expect To Achieve When Using LinkedIn Correctly

Networking is the driving force behind LinkedIn. Ultimately, outcomes that arise of being a LinkedIn member are direct results of networking. If used correctly, LinkedIn allows you the opportunity to boost your networking capabilities, helping you create a dedicated network that provides indefinite value for you and your career.

Traditional networking entails controlled environments, like a conference or industry-related event, where like-minded professionals can interact. With LinkedIn, individuals have the opportunity to further network with those individuals they've met. In the past, a lost business card meant a lost connection. Today, you can ensure that any person you've met can be contacted in the future.

LinkedIn can be thought of as a continual networking event in itself. Some connections that become part of your LinkedIn network will be people you've never actually met in person. While your LinkedIn network should closely mirror your offline network, there are many times when you expand your network by connecting with new, like-minded professionals.

With these expectations in place, one should view LinkedIn simply as a tool. The network that you build is just a byproduct of using the various features of LinkedIn. To understand how to use this immensely powerful networking tool, one first must understand the individual components that LinkedIn is comprised of. Once understood, best practices for leveraging these features can be examined.

Part Two: Understanding & Navigating The Components Of LinkedIn

This chapter lays the foundation for the rest of the book. We will explore the terminology specific to LinkedIn and how to navigate the platform. Many of these terms and concepts will be discussed in much further detail throughout the book.

LinkedIn Terminology

Connections: These are the people that you are connected with on LinkedIn. There are 3 levels of which you can be connected with another user. Connections are made when a member accepts your invitation to connect or when you've accepted an invitation from another member.

1st Degree Connections: These are those users that you have directly connected with via an invitation.

2nd Degree Connections: These are those users that are connections of your 1st degree connections.

3rd Degree Connections: These are those users that are connections of your 2nd degree connections.

Your Network: Your entire group of connections, regardless of the degree. Also group members are considered to be in your network. Members within your network are denoted by a symbol of their degree connection or a group symbol.

Out of Network: These are all LinkedIn members not within your network; they are denoted by an out of network tag next to their name.

Introductions: This feature allows members to bypass the limitations of connecting with members whose settings limit them from connecting. You can request an introduction to such person via one of your connections who's connected with him or her; there are limits on the amount of introductions each user has.

Profile: This is where you list all of your career information. This acts as your living, breathing resume within LinkedIn. Depending on your settings, you can allow anyone on the Internet to view your profile page and also dictate which information is shown depending on the viewer's level of connection to you.

Recommendations: These are references that you post about other members, and other members can post bout you. These will appear on your profile and are very important in letting others vouch for your abilities.

Skills Recommendations: In addition to recommendations, members can be recommended for individual skills. These skills will also appear on your profile. This allows members to pinpoint and recommend members based on certain skills.

Groups: Users are allowed to create and join groups, which are separate entities allowing members to interact around a certain industry, topic, or association.

Invitation: These are requests that you can either send or receive to make a first connection with another user.

Messages: Depending on the level of connection, you can message other members directly and they will receive your message in their LinkedIn inbox.

Update Feed: This is the page that displays all of your network's activity in a real time. This is similar to one's Facebook news feed.

InMail: These are private messages that allow members to send a message to any other member on LinkedIn. However, these are only made available to premium members and/or can be purchased by any member.

Update: Members are allowed to post updates that are broadcasted to their networks' update feed.

Settings: There are numerous settings for adjusting your networking experience. It is vital to understand what's controlled by these settings and how to optimally adjust them.

Company Page: Company pages are like profile pages, but for companies. They provide outlets for listing jobs, services, and posting company updates. Members can "follow" company pages to view updates in their update feed.

Influencer Feed: This is a separate update feed that only displays updates from the Influencers and Channels that you follow.

Influencer: An influencer is a person whose curated content can be subscribed to. Their content will appear in your Influencers feed.

Channel: These are curated topics suggested by LinkedIn such as marketing or technology, and made available to follow. Channel updates appear in the influencer feed.

OpenLink Network: Only offered to premium subscribers, the Openlink network allows members to freely contact all other Openlink members, without having to be connected.

Navigating The LinkedIn Terrain

From the homepage, you will be able to find and access all of the following areas of LinkedIn from the main navigation menu located in the top header area.

The Homepage
Once you've logged in to your account, you will be taken to your homepage. The homepage is the first option found in the main navigation bar. For those of you with a Facebook profile, the homepage is similar to your Facebook news stream.

LinkedIn will display information about the activity occurring within your network. You will be able to adjust your settings to control what content appears on your homepage. The next chapter walks you through these settings.

Many people confuse their homepage with their profile. Your profile is the static page containing all of the information just about you. Your homepage is a dynamic page that continually updates with information about your network.

Profile
The second tab listed in the main navigation is your profile. LinkedIn provides every user with a customizable profile. A mix between a business card, a resume, and a list of references, profiles provide users on outlet to boast about themselves, their skillsets, and past achievements.

Your LinkedIn profile is the most important component in regards to what you can control on LinkedIn, and is the best way to take grasp of your professional brand online. Those looking to learn more about you will come in contact with your profile; you have complete control of what is dictated. Part Four is dedicated just to creating a highly optimized profile.

Network

The third tab is your Network. By clicking on this link, you will be taken to a page where all of the connections you've made on LinkedIn are listed. There are sub navigation tabs that give you a few more options for adding new contacts to your network. These constantly change, but there is currently a page that is dedicated to viewing only alumni connections and a second page that helps you invite persons you know to join your network.

Jobs

The fourth tab takes you to the Jobs page. This page will help those looking for new career opportunities, as LinkedIn lists available jobs as paid for by the companies currently hiring. You can leverage advanced search filters to find jobs that best suit your needs.

Interests

The last tab in the navigation bar lists your Interests. There is no Interests page itself, just sub navigation tabs for the following features.

Companies

The company page lists all of the companies that you've chosen to follow. You will be able to visit this page for a stream of latest updates from only those companies you follow. Following companies is a great way to stay up-to-date with industry news and companies that may be of interest to you and your career.

Groups

The group page lists all of the groups you've joined. Groups are a great way to network with professionals that have similar interests to yours, and they provide the perfect outlet to share content, engage in discussion, offer services, and include a job bulletin for the posting of relevant jobs. Anybody can create their own group or join an already established group. You can join and be part of up to 50 groups at any given time.

Influencers

This newly added page acts as a stream of news and content specific to you. This is different than your homepage feed updates. LinkedIn allows you to follow "Channels" and "Influencers" as a way to curate a news stream that speaks to you. All of the updates and content shared by your channels and influencers will be streamed on this page.

Top Navigation Menu

These features are currently found in the top navigation menu, above the main navigation menu.

Message Inbox
Every user is designated their own message inbox; it's indicated by a message icon in the upper right corner of the top navigation menu. Messages, InMails, Group Invitations, and OpenLink messages will all be corralled into your inbox under the messages tab. Invitations are separated under their own tab within your inbox as well.

Notifications
The notification tab is listed next, as signified by a flag icon. It will be colored red whenever there is a new notification. Some actions that incite notifications include new invitations and new comments in discussions you are involved with.

Add Connections
Next, is an add connections tab as signified by a "person with a plus sign" icon. LinkedIn placed this tab here to remind users to continually strive to add new members to their networks. However, they try to get you to invite members not already part of LinkedIn – there is no significant usage for this tab. This tab is not how you find and engage with other users already on LinkedIn, as we will fully explore in Part Five.

Account & Settings
This last tab houses all of the administrative information such as your account type where they attempt to get you to upgrade your basic account. The most important link listed here is the link to your setting's page.

Search Bar & Advanced Search

The search bar is located in the middle of the top header. LinkedIn's search capabilities are far more powerful than most other social networks and search engines. The search bar will be most helpful in your daily tasks, such as finding your connections. LinkedIn also offers an advanced search page that offers tons of filters and tools for narrowing down results when you're in need of doing some serious digging.

Basic Search Bar
Basic search tasks can be conducted by using the search bar; this includes searching for users, groups, and companies for which you already know their name. The quickest way to bring up a connection's profile or a group you've joined is to just start typing in the name results will begin to appear instantly in a dropdown list below the search bar. If you don't see what you are looking for in these quickly returned results, hit enter and you will be taken to the advanced search page.

Advanced Search Page
The advanced search page will return all results that include the words you've entered into the search box. Entering "graphic design" into the search bar currently returns 2,136,548 results. These results include all possible matches, including people, jobs, companies, groups, updates, and even messages in your inbox that contain these keywords.

Depending on which results you are seeking, you can select any of these categorical result types on the left-hand side of the advanced search page. Once you've selected a result type, you will be shown additional filters for helping narrow down your results.

For example, if you are looking for a user, you will select "people" for your result type. Since you've selected "people", LinkedIn now provides filters to help further your search. Now, you will see the additional following filters appear:

Relationship, Location, Current Company, Industry, Past Company, School, and Profile Language. Using these filters you can construct an advanced search to find the exact user or type of user that you were searching for. Maybe you are looking for a graphic designer in the New York area, that has previously worked at a specific ad agency or went to NYU for graphic design. Using these search filters, you can find this exactly type of user.

In addition to search filters, you can use advanced search fields to narrow down results even further. At the top of the left hand sidebar you will find a link labeled "Advanced" with an arrow icon next to it. By selecting this link, a new menu will appear that provides additional search fields. These search fields include first name, last name, title, company, and zip code for which you can manually input any known information you have. The search filters will also be listed here for convenience, that way you can use both search filters and search fields at once, delivering you with highly targeted results.

Connecting With Other Users

Similar to the premise of any other social network, connecting with other users is the driving force and main incentive for joining LinkedIn. Just as Facebook allows you to "friend" others and Twitter allows you to "follow" others, LinkedIn has created it its own unique system for member interaction. You can "connect" with other users; there are three levels of connectivity. In addition to connection levels, there are alternative networking features, such as groups, where you can interact with other members without having to directly "connect" with.

This section is very important. The connection level with another member dictates which networking features and settings take precedence. Once you begin growing your network, you will see firsthand how these different degrees of connectivity influence your capabilities to network.

Degrees Of Connections

Every member on LinkedIn is either classified as within your network or outside of your network. If they are inside of your network, there are three degrees for which they can be connected.

1st Degree Connections – These are the people you are directly connected with. You will see a symbol next to their name stating they are a 1st degree connection.

2nd Degree Connections – These are the people that are directly connected with one of your 1st degree connections. You will see a symbol next to their name stating they are a 2nd degree connection.

3rd Degree Connections – These are the people that are directly connected with one of your 2nd degree connections. You will see a symbol next to their name stating they are a 3rd degree connection.

Outside of these three major connection levels, there's an additional way for users to be considered inside of your network. If you are a member of a Group, all other group members will be considered part of your network. You will see a symbol next to their name indicating they are a Group connection. If you have a 1st degree connection with any group member, that connection will take precedence and they will be listed as a 1st degree connection.

Members that do not fall within any of these connection classifications will be considered outside of your network. There will be a small notification next to their name that displays "Out of your network".

Like most features of LinkedIn, connecting with other users is a fairly easy process; the basic account allows you to seamlessly navigate the platform. However, there are certain features made available to only premium LinkedIn members. Most all users can utilize the basic account to garner a highly powered network, especially after reading all of the tips and strategies supplied in this book. It is important that we look the premium subscription levels currently offered by LinkedIn, as the features and permissions of these accounts will help paint a bigger picture of what users are fully capable of accomplishing on LinkedIn.

Premium Account Subscriptions

There are numerous subscription types within LinkedIn and each account type offers unique features or extended use of the features made available to the basic accounts. Due to the ever evolving employment landscape, LinkedIn continues to change the features of each subscription level and also create new types to better aid its' users. Ultimately, premium subscriptions provide a tailored experience to users, making it easier to achieve success within LinkedIn.

Regardless of how you intend to use LinkedIn, mostly all features are made available in the basic (free) account. Upgrading to a premium account will provide you with a few new features to use, but mostly it will just allow you more bandwidth when using the basic features. However, it's important to note the few feature differences amongst the paid subscriptions, as these subtleties may be give you the boost needed to help you achieve your goals more efficiently.

Of the five account types, "Basic", "LinkedIn Premium", and "LinkedIn for Job Seekers" are the ones worth noting. The other two subscription types are designed specifically for Sales Professionals and Recruiters. Unless you work within either of these industries or in a position where recruiting and sales responsibilities are assigned to you, these are not worth exploring further.

From a bird's eye view, lets look at the 5 Account types currently offered:

Basic (Free)
The basic account is sufficient for most professionals. It provides almost all features offered by LinkedIn; it just limits the extent of which you can use a few of the features. Unless you're a highly active user who wants the ability to reach out to many members outside of your network, the basic account is all that you will need.

LinkedIn Premium

LinkedIn premium is simply a more powerful basic account. All features provided in the basic account are again provided with the premium account, with the addition of a few new features and extended access to the basic features. The only difference worth noting here is the additional messaging capabilities, which allow one to contact users outside of their network through use of InMails. Basic members can upgrade their account to premium at anytime (and also downgrade back to free).

LinkedIn Premium should be considered for those professionals that will routinely need to reach outside of their networks for business purposes / work in a sales type position.

LinkedIn For Job Seekers

For job seekers, an efficient job search starts by tapping into one's own network. However, there will be many times where reaching outside of one's network is crucial. Contacting HR professionals, recruiters, and persons at a certain company will require increased messaging capabilities.

Similar to LinkedIn Premium, the Job Seekers account includes increased messaging capabilities via InMail messages. Additionally, when applying to jobs listed on the LinkedIn job board, Linked Job Seekers' applications are given priority and show up first in the digital pile of applications.

For those users in the midst of job searching, applying to jobs, and gathering more information about companies and positions, the LinkedIn for Job Seekers account may provide an additional boost. LinkedIn Premium may choose to be a more economically sound choice because you will receive increased InMail usage at the same price point.

However, if you will be actively applying to jobs through the LinkedIn Job Board, the Job Seekers subscription may make more sense because your job applications receive priority when submitted to employers.

LinkedIn For Recruiters
With so many professionals flocking to LinkedIn, the recruiting industry had no choice but to follow the herd. A quick candidate search on LinkedIn now reaps the same rewards as hours of cold calling once did. This is the account that I (Jonathan) currently use for my recruiting efforts; I couldn't do my job without this account.

The Recruiter Account provides several features that recruiters benefit immensely from. Messaging capabilities are increased such as with the Premium and Job Seeker accounts. More importantly, this account enables recruiters to see all of a person's listed information, as long as they are within their network (1st, 2nd, 3rd degree connections & group members). Basic members can usually only see profile information of their 1st connections.

This is a very powerful feature when in the hands of a recruiter. If I can connect with one person at a given company, then I will immediately gain access to all information listed on the profiles of all of this person's colleagues.

While we recruiters do send a lot of Inmails and messages to possible candidates, it's more important that we can read about the users that come up in our searches. It's a waste of time sending an Inmail to somebody whose name and information are only partially shown. A while back, my network consisted of around 400 1st degree connections, providing me an entire network size of 9.4 Million members, meaning I could view the entire profile of almost 10 Million members. LinkedIn for Recruiters is ideal for any recruiter, heavily rewarding those who can aggressively build a network surrounding the job types they recruit for.

LinkedIn For Sales Professionals

Similar to LinkedIn Premium and LinkedIn for Recruiters, this account allows for greater outreach capabilities. The biggest difference is that this accounts allows for more Introductions than Inmails, which is ideal for Sales persons.

The most successful salespersons build up their client base through referral business; using Introductions is LinkedIn's way of empowering referral business. While direct messaging through Inmails may seem like a better ploy, less invasive Introductions make for better outreach strategy. This account is ideal for Sales Professionals who understand the importance of referral business and are looking to leverage their network online.

What Exactly Does Each Subscription Provide?
Within these 5 subscription types, there are various levels at which one could subscribe to. For example, there are 3 levels of commitment to choose from within the Premium Job Seeker Subscription: Job Seeker basic, Job Seeker, and Job Seeker Plus.

Access to all of the same features is usually found at subscription level, the difference being the amount of allowed usage increased with each level. For example Job Seeker Plus provides users with 10 InMails a month, whereas Job Seeker only provides users with 5 InMails.

Pricing is based on a monthly plan, but annual rates are also offered. You can find the exact pricing and details breakdown of each Account Types here:
http://help.LinkedIn.com/app/answers/detail/a_id/71

Although each account type is summarized above, below is a condensed list of the notable features. You can see what features come with the different accounts. The table only lists the 3 accounts of which most people will utilize– Basic, Premium, and Job Seeker.

Again, it's important to note that there are different levels of subscription available within the Premium and Job Seeker account types. It's up to the individual to decide how much bandwidth they will need. You can always change your subscription type and the level of subscription at any time.

This chart is subject to change, we advise you to visit LinkedIn for the most current subscription options and pricing. This is just a quick reference for most readers, as premium subscription is neither mandatory nor promoted in this book. Below you will find quick definitions of the features – this is informative for all readers, regardless of what account subscription you use.

Feature	Basic	Premium	Job Seeker
Who's Viewed Your profile	Limited	Yes	Yes
See full profiles of everyone in your network	Limited	Yes	Yes
See full names of 3rd degree and group connections	Limited	Yes (highest subscription level)	Yes (highest subscription level)
InMail Messages	No	3, 10, 25 (Across the 3 subscription levels)	0, 5, 10 (Across the 3 subscription levels)
Introductions	5	15, 25, 35 (Across the 3 subscription levels)	10,15,25 (Across the 3 subscription levels)
OpenLink	No	Yes	Yes

Premium Search	No	4,4,8 (Across the 3 subscription levels)	N/A
Profiles Per Search	100	300, 500, 700 (Across the 3 subscription levels)	N/A
Saved Search Alerts	3	5, 7, 10 (Across the 3 subscription levels)	N/A
Featured Applicant	No	No	Yes
Premium Badge	No	Yes	Yes
Job Seeker Group and Webinar	No	No	Yes
Profile Organizer	No	Yes	Yes

Who's Viewed Your Profile

This feature allows you to see who has viewed your profile. This is very helpful in discovering who may be interested in your skillsets, business, or someone who may have a career opportunity. It even provides the keywords people used to find you and stats about who they are. This information is helpful in refining your profile to include keywords that are already bringing visitors your way

See Full profiles of Everyone in Your Network

This feature allows you to see the entire profile of any of your 1st, 2nd, and 3rd degree connections.

See Full Names of 3rd Degree and Group Connections

This feature allows you to see the full names of any connections in your Network, including those that are just connected via a shared Group.

InMail Messages
This feature allows you to send InMails. InMails allow you to contact anybody on LinkedIn, regardless of whether they are part of your network or not. It is important to note that InMails can be purchased directly as well, without having to upgrade your account. Currently, LinkedIn sells InMails for $10 each.

Introductions
This feature allows you to initiate conversation with a user for which you can't connect with due to your connection level or his/her settings.

OpenLink Network
This feature allows you to become a member of the OpenLink network, which allows any LinkedIn member to send you a FREE InMail message. This will allow for more members to get in touch with you because it allows basic members the ability to InMail you without having to pay.

Premium Search
This feature allows for even greater search capabilities within LinkedIn's search engine. There are 4 advanced search filters, which include company size, interests, seniority, and Fortune 1000. There are four more premium search filters that include groups, years of experience, new to LinkedIn, and functions that are provided for Premium members that subscribe to the highest level.

Profiles Per Search
This feature allows for more profiles to appear in your search results.

Saved Search Alerts

This feature will allow you to save your search criteria for discovering new professionals to network with. You will be sent notifications of when new users join that meet your search criteria.

Featured Applicant

The feature guarantees that your application to a job on the LinkedIn Job Board is seen first by the person who posted the job.

Premium Badge

This feature allows for an optional badge to be displayed next to your name. There are two types: premium and job seeker. The premium badge helps your profile stand out and implies that you have access to Inmails and advanced networking features. The Job Seeker badge implies that you are seeking opportunities, which may help catch the eye of a hiring manager.

Job Seeker Group and Webinar

This feature entitles users to helpful job search webinars held by LinkedIn and includes membership to a specific group for job seekers.

Profile Organizer

This feature allows you to keep track of any profiles you come across. Using folders and notes to categorize your connections, you will always have information handy that may be helpful in the future.

Regardless of your account type, the networking and best practices instruction in the upcoming chapters will be applicable for all users. The next chapter focuses on properly adjusting settings to improve networking capabilities.

Part Three: Optimizing Account Settings To Facilitate Better Networking

Before optimizing our profiles, it's mandatory that we understand the settings controlling our LinkedIn Accounts. There are extensive amounts of settings for which you can control. Similar to Facebook, Twitter, and other social networks, there are various privacy settings that control how your content is displayed across your network.

With LinkedIn being the professional network, privacy settings and permissions should be at an utmost priority for you and the professionals in your network. Thus, LinkedIn provides tight controls for which every user should take the time to learn and adjust based on their intentions. We want to adjust these settings to help facilitate your networking efforts, not hinder them.

There are times when you want your interactions to be viewed, such as the sharing of an opportunity with your network, or a company blog post that may help drive visitors to the company's page. However, this is not always the case.

Employees, currently unhappy with their position, may want to interact in Group discussions and connect with recruiters at other companies. These job seekers would certainly not want all of this activity publicly displayed across the Home Update Feeds of their connections (coworkers and bosses!).

Let's dissect the current settings made available by LinkedIn.

Accessing The Settings Area

Once logged in to your account, you will find the Privacy & Settings tab listed in the top right hand navigation. A dropdown tab listed under the image thumbnail of your profile picture will display the Privacy & Settings tab. Once you click on this tab, you will be taken to your settings page that appears as such:

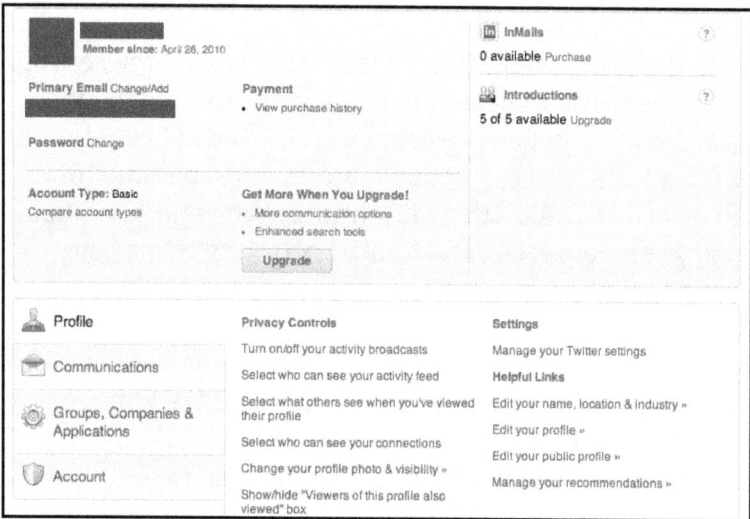

The larger box at the top lists some basic information about your account such as the date you joined LinkedIn, your email and password, your account type, and the current number of available InMails and Introductions at your disposal.

Below this box, you will find all of your settings organized into 4 Tabs:

- Your Profile
- Communications
- Groups, Companies, and Communications
- Account

Within each tab, you will find settings that control important aspects of your networking experience. LinkedIn inserts additional links into each of these tabs that do not control any settings, but are merely reference links for which you may find helpful. We will focus on just the important settings within each tab and simply make note of the additional links LinkedIn inserts.

Slight adjustments to many of these settings can completely alter your networking experience on LinkedIn, so it's important to look through your settings intently.

Your Profile Settings

Profile	Privacy Controls	Settings
Communications	Turn on/off your activity broadcasts	Manage your Twitter settings
	Select who can see your activity feed	Helpful Links
Groups, Companies & Applications	Select what others see when you've viewed their profile	Edit your name, location & industry »
	Select who can see your connections	Edit your profile »
Account	Change your profile photo & visibility »	Edit your public profile »
	Show/hide "Viewers of this profile also viewed" box	Manage your recommendations »

Within the Profile tab, you will see a column marked Privacy Controls on the left side. These settings will impact how your profile is displayed, and who can access the information listed on your profile. On the right side, you will find two categories: Settings and Helpful Links. The only one worth mentioning is the "Manager your Twitter Settings" link, as this allows you to list your Twitter handle on your profile. Let's focus on the left column, Privacy Controls, and walk through how adjustments should be made to these settings.

Privacy Controls

Turn on/off your activity broadcasts

This setting controls broadcasts of certain activities you partake in; you have the option to disable activity such as profile changes, made recommendations, and following companies. These broadcasts will be listed in the activity feed on your profile. We suggest turning this option off, especially if you are actively job searching, as you may not want your current employer to visit your profile and see that you are quite active.

Select who can see your activity feed
Your activity feed displays recent actions you've performed on LinkedIn. You can select which users can view your activity feed; you can select everyone, just your connections, or only you. If your activity broadcasts are on (see first setting), be careful in selecting those who can see your activity. There is an

upside for allowing others to see your activity feed, as some of your actions may be relevant to onlookers, which may trigger a potential career opportunity.

Select what others see when you've viewed their profile
When you look at other users' profiles, they will be notified of this. You have the three options for how they will be notified of your viewing:
1- Your profile picture thumbnail, name, and headline will be shown
2- Only profile characteristics, such as industry and title are shown
3- A completely anonymous profile will be shown.

By selecting either of the last two options, the ability for you to see who's viewed your profile is disabled. Since networking is an action that involves other people, it is recommended that you allow your profile picture, name, and headline to be shown (1st option). In return, you will get to see who's viewed your profile, which is very useful information when it comes to building your network.

Select who can see your connections
You can opt to display your connections on your profile. It is highly recommended that you allow your connections to be displayed, as this helps those in your network discover and communicate with similar connections. By allowing your connections to network with one another, you will be providing much value to your network with very little effort.

Change your profile photo & visibility
This links you to a page where you can edit your profile image. Additionally, you have the option to select who can view it. You can make your profile image viewable to your connections, your network, or everyone. Setting this to "everyone" is recommended, but selecting your network is fine as well. You just want your 2nd and 3rd connections to be able to put a face to your name in case they've met you or meet you in the future.

Show/hide "Viewers of this profile also viewed" box
This option, if selected, will display a box on your profile that shows visitors other user profiles that may be of interest. It's suggested that you disable this option as to remove clutter from your profile and maintain viewer focus on you, as it's your profile page.

Your Communications Settings

Profile	**Emails and Notifications**	**LinkedIn Communications**
Communications	Set the frequency of emails	Turn on/off invitations to participate in research
Groups, Companies & Applications	Set push notification settings	Turn on/off partner InMail
Account	**Member Communications**	
	Select the types of messages you're willing to receive	
	Select who can send you invitations	

In the left column you will find two categories, Emails and Notifications and Member Communications, and these are again important settings one must consider adjusting. In the right column, there are just 2 links under the category LinkedIn Communications. These are just for optional newsletters, promotional partners, and research surveys that LinkedIn opts you into by default. You can disable both of these if you wish to not get bothered by such promotion.

Let's look at the settings in the left column:

Emails and Notifications

Set the frequency of emails
This is an extremely useful setting, as you can control which LinkedIn notifications will trigger an email and at what frequency. Instead of getting a notification every time a user sends you an invitation to connect, you can choose to receive a weekly email notification with all of your invitations.

These settings will save you the time and headache of digging through your inbox or being bothered by insignificant notifications. Currently, you can enable/disable email notifications and/or their frequency of these types of email notifications: Messages, invitations, updates in your network, all of your different group activities, insights from LinkedIn, and other notifications in response to your activity.

Set push notification settings
If you download and use the LinkedIn app, which is a highly we highly suggest doing (see resources section for links to the app), you can control which notifications will trigger a push message to your mobile devices.

Member Communications

Select the types of message you're willing to receive
This is another important setting where you control the types of message that are sent your way. You can disable all messaging types, except Invitations and Messages from your 1st Degree connections.

It is not recommended that you disarm other user from communicating with you. For some users this may be extremely useful, such as those with high in-demand skills such as programmers or highly esteemed executives, who would otherwise get bombarded with InMails everyday. You can also select specific opportunities for which you would be receptive to and these selections will appear on your Public Profile. This can be left blank as it offers no real value, and most viewers will never see this information as it's listed on the bottom of your Public Profile.

Select who can send you invitations
The last setting can adjust who's allowed to send you invitations in an effort to establish a 1st Degree connection.

There are 3 options:
- Anyone on LinkedIn
- People who know your email address or appear in your "Imported Contacts" list
- Only people who appear in your "Imported Contacts" list.

Your imported contacts list is all of the contacts you may have optionally imported by email; this list helps you sort of prequalify any of your contacts so they can reach out to you and find you more easily once they join Linkedin.

By default, any one on LinkedIn can now send you an invite to connect. You should leave this setting untouched, as you can always reject or ignore invitations.

Your Groups, Companies & Applications Settings

Profile	Groups	Applications
Communications	Select your group display order »	View your applications »
	View your groups »	Add applications »
Groups, Companies & Applications	Set the frequency of group digest emails	**Privacy Controls**
	Turn on/off group invitations	Turn on/off data sharing with 3rd party applications
Account	Turn on/off notifications when joining groups	Manage settings for LinkedIn plugins on third-party sites
	Companies	
	View companies you're following »	

In the third tab, you will find several settings that control your Groups and Companies preferences in the left column. On the right side, you will find settings for third party Applications and privacy controls of such third party access points.

Don't get overwhelmed. This tab contains a lot of different settings, but these settings have little impact on how you and your actions appear across LinkedIn. It is good to understand what these settings allow you to control, but not crucial to your networking proficiency.

Groups

Select your group display order
This lets you order the listing of your groups on you Groups page. This may help you prioritize your top groups just so you can find them quicker, nothing else.

View your groups
This is just a link to your Groups page.

Set the frequency of group digest emails
This is a very important setting. You can control if and how often you will receive digest emails from groups you are a member of. You can select never, daily, or weekly. This is a very efficient way of eliminated tons of group emails that you are automatically signed up for once joining a group.

However, you can't control the option of receiving messages from group managers in this section. You must visit each group's settings page individually to further adjust these messaging options.

Turn on/off group invitations
You can control whether other users can send you invitations to join a group. You should not disable this option, as many of your connections will ask you to join groups that further discussion around topics you probably be of interest.

Turn on/off notifications when joining groups
This is another important setting. You can control whether or not your network will get shown an update in their feed of you joining a new group. For job seekers, you should certainly turn notifications off, especially if you are joining groups that would signify a career change.

At the bottom of the column, you will find the Companies section; there is only one listed resource link in this section. This is a simple link to your company page where all of the companies you are currently following are listed.

In the right column, you will find the Applications and Privacy Controls Sections:

Applications

View Your Applications
By clicking on this link, you will be taken to a page that lists all of the "Applications" and "External Websites" you've given permission to.

Applications
Prior to a new update from LinkedIn, there were many "Applications" that users could install to enhance their profiles. This allowed for the inclusion of YouTube or documents from SlideShare right into one's profile.

Now, while these capabilities still exist, "apps" are no longer the vehicle allowing these enhancements. LinkedIn has improved their native capabilities so users can take advantage of all of these third party applications without having to actually install apps. Although still in release, LinkedIn has approved many content providers, such as SlideShare and Pinterest for example, to become integrated into the content sharing experience.

Here is a current list of media providers that have been approved by LinkedIn.
http://help.LinkedIn.com/app/answers/detail/a_id/34327

LinkedIn is in the early stages of integration, allowing users to enhance their profiles with such media or embed such content into updates and group discussion. Stay tuned as LinkedIn continuously adds new content providers to it's approved list.

With that being said, "Apps" haven't completely disappeared, but their usage is no longer needed. If you had used such apps in the past, they may be found under this "Applications" column, otherwise you may only see a Polls Application, which is one that LinkedIn itself has made. While this may be confusing, it may interest some readers who had experience dealing with Apps in the past.

External Websites
This column lists any third party websites that you have granted permission to use your LinkedIn information. Maybe you've connected your LinkedIn profile to signup for another website, or have allowed another site to pull your information from LinkedIn. Any website, for which this was allowed, is listed here. You can remove any of these permissions if you no longer use the third party website or rather not have your LinkedIn information shared.

Add Applications

Since applications are now a thing of the past, LinkedIn has replaced this setting with a link to this page:

http://help.linkedin.com/app/answers/detail/a_id/34324

This just explains the new update, which we've just discussed, helping users understand the change and what new capabilities will me possible.

Privacy Controls
There are two Privacy Controls settings controlling how your personal data is shared with Applications and External Websites.

Turn on/off data sharing with 3rd party applications
LinkedIn may continue to build it's own applications such as the Polls app, so it's best that you allow data sharing so any new apps introduced can be utilized.

Manage settings for LinkedIn plugins on third-party sites
The second setting specifically pertains to LinkedIn Plugins, such as LinkedIn Sharing buttons used on blogs. Enabling this setting allows and offsite activity to be shared with LinkedIn so they can better tailor your experience when you are on their platform. This allows LinkedIn to keep tabs of any interaction you may have with third party websites. These third party websites are those that have integrated LinkedIn components into their experience such as sharing buttons and login credentials. If concerned about this data being shared, go ahead and disable this setting.

Your Account Settings

Profile	Privacy Controls	Email & Password
	Manage Advertising Preferences	Add & change email addresses
Communications	Settings	Change password
	Change your profile photo & visibility »	Helpful Links
Groups, Companies & Applications	Show/hide profile photos of other members	Upgrade your account »
	Customize the updates you see on your home page	Close your account »
Account		Get LinkedIn content in an RSS feed »
	Select your language	
	Manage security settings	

The last tab contains your Account settings. These settings are important in regards to your overall account. Again, there are several links simply placed here for easy reference, addressing many common questions users have about their account.

In the left column, you will find two categories: Privacy Controls and Settings.

Privacy Controls

There use to be much controversy surrounding some of the advertising and privacy controls, which is usually the case with any website. LinkedIn has done a good job responding to the controversy and has removed questionable practices that are not worth discussing here.

There is one remaining control:

Manage Advertising Preferences
This just states LinkedIn's policy and how they no do not share your information with advertisers. You have the option to grant LinkedIn permission to show you Ads on third party websites. There isn't much documentation on this setting from a users standpoint, so disable if concerned. This should ultimately free you of "retargeted ads" from companies trying to show you their Ad on those websites you visit after leaving LinkedIn.

Settings

Change your profile photo & visibility
This will link you to your profile picture page where you can edit your photo. Your settings allow you to make your picture visible to just your connections, your network, or everyone.

Show/hide profile photos of other members
This setting allows you to select whose picture you will see when on LinkedIn. Here, you can choose to see the profile pictures of your connections, your network, everyone, or no one.

Customize the updates you see on your home page
This setting will trigger a pop up box containing many settings. You will be able to select the exact updates you wish to see appear in your home feed. Take advantage of this setting to tailor your home page experience to only show you things that will be of benefit to you. Currently, there are 10 options for which you can select to be shown in your home feed. You can also select how many updates are shown at once.

Select your language
Simply select the language you wish LinkedIn to appear in.

Manage security settings
This single option allows you to enable a more secure connection point. It's suggested that you enable the setting "use a secure connection (https) to browse LinkedIn", as it will better protect you when using a non-secure internet connection for if and when you are at a café or public library.

Email & Password

Add & change email addresses
This setting will ask you to enter in a 2nd email to be tied to your account. It is recommended that you enter in a 2nd email address, as many people only enter in their work email and

lose access to that email account when they change jobs. By adding a personal email, you will never get locked out of your account if your work email is deactivated. You can select which of the two emails will be your primary email, and this will be the one that receives notification emails.

Change password
This is the setting for changing your current password.

Helpful Links

Upgrade your account
This will send you to the subscription page where you can upgrade your basic Account to a paid account.

Close your account
This link will send you to a page where you can ask to have your account closed.

Get LinkedIn content in an RSS feed
This link will send you to a page where you can turn your network updates into an RSS feed.

Part Four: Building & Optimizing Your Profile

We've finally at arrived at the most central component of your LinkedIn network, You! Your LinkedIn profile gives you an incredible opportunity to accurately depict your career and exhibit your professional ambitions. Think of your LinkedIn profile as a living, breathing resume (as long as you keep it updated!).

Gone are the days of static resumes. LinkedIn continues to roll out profile enhancement options, such as skill endorsements and the inclusion of rich media (slides, video, audio), giving users new ways to boast and brag about career achievements. Regardless of the new features being rolled out, you will always have final say on how your profile is assembled.

New features such as skill endorsements allow others to interact with your profile. While your connections will be able to recommend the skills you've listed on your profile, you can opt to show/not show these endorsements. Removing these endorsements from your profile wouldn't make sense, but the point is that you have complete control of what is displayed on your profile.

When building **YOUR** profile, it's time to get selfish. Just as sharing, giving, and deferring to others is so instrumental in Networking, bragging needs to be the de facto motive when crafting your profile.

You learned how to build websites with Wordpress? Add that skill to your profile.

You just completed an intense 18-month project for an international business development group? Add this project to your profile

Any skill set, certification, project, accomplishment, book you've authored, or job you've held that would be conceived as valuable to your intended audience should be included in your profile.

Similar to building a resume, there's a right and wrong way to building a LinkedIn profile. Since LinkedIn profiles are dynamic, index able by LinkedIn and search engines, and responsive in displaying information to your various connections, crafting a profile is a much more intensive task than typing a static resume. Fortunately, LinkedIn makes editing your profile very easy. You can always update/alter your profile, so don't be hesitant to include new features because nothing is permanent.

Building Your Profile

The most important aspect of building your profile is that it must accurately reflect who you are as a professional. Adding fluff, industry buzzwords, and lies to your profile will only endanger future career opportunities and cause mistrust amongst your network of connections. Since we are looking to build a highly personalized network full of likeminded professionals, one that will be fruitful for years to come, honesty and integrity must be take center stage in our profiles.

However, building an accurate and transparent profile is just the start; we need to optimize our profiles to stand out in front of the other 200 million or so profiles registered with LinkedIn. Odds are, some of these members share your same profession, location, and skillset. There may be 50 professionals in your city with the exact same work experience and skillsets, but only 10 of these persons will show up on the first page of search results. According to click through rate statistics, 84% of users click 1st page results.

So how do you become one of the users to appear in the first page of search results for various industry and skill specific keyword searches?

LinkedIn's algorithm, as well as search engines such as Google, return results based on keywords found in your profile. This is brings us to the second aspect of building a great profile, specificity.

The key is to be as specific as possible when crafting your profile. While it would be great to be the first user listed in search results for the keyword "sales", the lack of specificity reaps little reward. However, if you are the user that appears first for the term "Dallas B2B sales professional", visitors of your profile will have found exactly who they were looking for.

In this chapter, we first look at the current composition of a LinkedIn profile. A quick overview of the profile components and terminology will help us understand what actually needs to be optimized.

Next, we will look to optimize each of these components. We will cover best practices for gaining more visibility for our profiles. These strategies will increase visibility within both LinkedIn's search engine and other search engines.

Lastly, we will discuss the difference between your profile and your public profile. Settings for your public profile differ from the settings discussed in the last chapter; these public profile settings control how you appear when people using search engines come across your profile.

Profile Layout

This section is just a quick snapshot of all the components our profiles are composed of. With countless other profiles demanding the same attention we are, it's imperative that we enlist all of the features available to strengthen our profile.

To visit your profile page, head to the profile tab in the main navigation menu. Once on your profile screen, select the grey box that says, "Edit profile" from within your main header.

This will place you into edit mode, and you can now edit every section of your profile. For quick reference, here is the list of editable profile components. In the next section, we reference each of these components when making our optimizations. These profile components, and the instruction in the next section, are both ordered top to bottom by appearance in your profile.

1. **Name, Professional Headline, Location and Industry** – Where you list basic profile information that users come across when finding your profile listing
2. **Profile Picture** – Where you insert a professional headshot or photo
3. **Contact Info** - Email, IM, Phone Number, Address, Twitter, Websites
4. **Activity** – Your status updates and recent activity
5. **Recommended For You - Additional Sections Add To Your profile** - Current options include Languages,

Publications, Organizations, Honors & Awards, as well as certifications, courses, patents, test scores, and volunteering.

6. **Profile Summary** – Your professional elevator pitch, where discuss your career achievements and ambitions.

7. **Experience** – Where you add your current and past work experience

8. **Upload A File or Add A Link** – Add links or rich media to you Summary, Experience, and Projects

9. **Skills & Expertise** – Where you can list your specific skills and your connections can endorse you for those skills

10. **Education** – Where you list all formal schooling information

11. **Additional Info** – Interests, Personal Info, and Advice for Contacting You

12. **Recommendations** – Written recommendations provided by your connections

13. **Connections** – Listing of all of your first connections

14. **Groups** - A Listing of your current group associations

15. **Following** – Currently You Can Follow LinkedIn News Verticals and Individual Companies

Optimizing Your Profile (15 Steps)

With reference to all of the components mentioned in the last section, let's now get into the meat and potatoes of this book – optimizing our profiles for networking success. It's best practice to follow this guide in order, cross-referencing suggestions for each component with your own profile.

1. Name, Professional Headline, Location and Industry

Name

While it may seem obvious to use your real name here, many people get cute and use a pseudo name or first and middle name. Remember, this is not Facebook or Twitter. This is the professional network. Since you network with real people, get hired by real people, and sign your W-2 for real HR people, make sure to use your real name.

Professional Headline

Not so obvious is the professional headline. The headline is one of the most important aspects of your profile. It's what shows up in search results for when others are either specifically looking for you, or someone with your skillset/background.

Most people just put their current position title in the headline – something like, "Account Manager at XYZ". While true, it doesn't reflect what you do exactly. An account manager could mean a lot of different things. Also, by including a company's name in YOUR headline, you are discounting your own professional existence. While it's great promotion for your company, it's not great branding for your own behalf. We will discuss our current positions in the experience area of our profile, but not in the headline.

A great headline includes your specific skillsets and expertise in relation to your industry. These keywords should be what people use when searching for individuals like you. Are you unsure of what keywords to include?

Enter keywords relevant to your skills and experience into the LinkedIn search bar. Take note of the first few profiles that appear in each search and see what other keywords are being included in their headlines. This may take some time, but it's important to find the most appropriate words used by industry leaders.

Do not use big buzzwords like "marketer", "connector", "leader", as nobody searches for these. Remember, specificity is crucial; people search with specific intent. Instead of the buzzwords just listed, people search "search engine optimization specialist", "international business development", and "fortune 500 sales manger". Career opportunities will increase, if and when your profile comes up first in a highly targeted search such as "search engine optimization specialist", rather than "marketer".

You may include your company's name at the end of your headline if it helps with credibility among your industry or if you want to bring attention to your own company, but generally you will include this info elsewhere in your profile.

Note to jobseekers – DO NOT PUT " Seeking Opportunity" here or something of that sort! Employers are looking for highly talented, highly desired employees, not those who are desperately job searching. As a recruiter, there are very few things as off-putting than to see these types of headlines. You are not describing anything that you bring to the table other than availability. While seeking top talent, it's very easy to ignore these types of profiles.

Location
When editing your location, you will be asked for your Zip Code. Once entered, LinkedIn will suggest a few locations to choose from. It's best to select the location that is broadest. While you could choose New York, New York as your location, it's better to select the Greater New York Area. When given the

opportunity, choose the larger area because professionals may be unfamiliar with you're exact city if it's a smaller one.

Industry
Select the industry that most accurately reflects your profession and not your company's industry. An HR professional working at American Express should not select Financial Services just because they work for a large financial company. They should select Human Resources as their industry. Base your industry selection around your career, and not that of the company you work for.

2. Profile Picture

First, you need a profile picture. Second, you need a picture that is professional and of high quality. It's best to format your picture to this size of 500pixels x 500 pixels, as the dimensions will remain intact when reduced for your thumbnail picture (the small picture that appears in search results). When you interact with others, whether online or offline, first impression means everything. If you don't have a picture for your profile, or display an unprofessional photo, you may be raising some red flags.

Once you've selected a picture, you will have the option as to who can see your picture. Options include making your profile photo visible to just your connections, your entire network, or everyone. It's best that you choose either your network or everyone, as you want to build trust with anybody looking to conduct future business that may not already be a direct connection.

By enabling your picture to be seen across your entire network, someone may recognize you from a networking event, blog post, or anywhere else you have a presence. This allows group members, not directly connected with you, to see your picture and this may encourage them to invite you to become a 1st degree connection.

3. Contact Info

Email, IM, Phone Number, Address, Twitter, Websites
This area is hidden by default to onlookers of your profile, with only 1st degree connections allowed to unhide all information. Your website and twitter accounts can be seen by everyone else.

It's important to enter in contact info as it will help those who've you connected with get in touch. You can leave out your phone number and address, as these can be passed along to your connections if needed.

You can enter in up to 3 websites for display in your contact info. This is a great place to add one of your own websites or blogs. Don't spend too much time in this section, as it is not a highly visited area of your profile because it's minimized by default to onlookers. It is a great way to place some more industry keywords to help boost the optimization of your profile for these keywords. Only include these keywords if you can appropriately include them.

4. Activity

The activity section is always visible to you and lists any of your recent actions. LinkedIn considers adding new jobs, schools, website links, recommendations, following companies, adding connections, and status updates as activity to appear in this activity stream. You can control who can see this activity stream and what appears in the settings area, as we've already discussed.

5. Recommended For You - Additional Sections Add To Your profile

We want to make our profiles as robust as possible. By adding more information, we increase our profile's chances of appearing in more search results for various search terms. On the right hand side, you will find a library of add-on sections. These options currently include Languages, Publications, Organizations, Honors & Awards, as well as Certifications, Courses, Patents, Test Ccores, and Volunteering.

Most users ignore these lesser-known profile add-ons, so enlisting a few of these components gives us an edge. If you know more than 1 language, you can now separately highlight this in your profile. If you belong to a well-recognized organization within your industry, you can now separately highlight this in your profile. While before it was best practice to include all of this information throughout our profiles, we can now enlist these designated sections to help us organize our bragging.

Only include the add-on sections that will add value to your profile. Just because there is an option for test scores doesn't mean you have to include it. If you have passed an intense financial or accounting examination, include this score. If you only have an SAT score from 20 years ago, keep this to yourself.

Filling out the required information for the add-ons is quite self-explanatory. The Languages, Publications, Organizations, Honors & Awards, Certifications, Courses, Patents, Test scores, and Volunteering add-ons will prompt you for information once you select to include them by clicking the plus button (+). Once inserted in your profile, you can rearrange the order of where they are positioned. We discuss how to do this at the end of this section.

6. Profile Summary

The profile summary is one of the most important aspects of your profile. It is essentially a blank canvas, positioned at the top of your profile, giving you a chance to grab visitors' attention. Think of it as your "elevator speech".

"What do you do?" "Why should I care?" Here is where you will answer these questions. You have up to 2000 characters (although we will use much less) to differentiate yourself from the next professional. The summary area and headline, offer the most flexibility and opportunity to capture visitors' attention.

Your summary appears "above the fold". This means that when visitors come across your profile, they don't have to scroll down the page to find it. While other areas of your profile are important, visitors will never see these areas if they aren't captivated by your summary.

A great summary increases the odds that visitors will take the time to read through your experience, recommendations, and listed skills; these are the crucial area of your profile for convincing them that you are the person they need in their network.

Where traditional resumes provide little space to include anything other than objective, factual information, your profile summary allows you to position yourself within the industry and highlight your career turning points. A great summary should be written with the reader in mind, although we will also include keywords to appease the search engines.

Great Profile Summaries Include:

A Great Story
People love stories, and they love short stories. Here's your chance to tell your story. This is where you can separate yourself from the other candidates who also have 5+ years experience, know how to use Sales Force, and have worked as a sales manager. Most times, the top candidates for my positions are all equally qualified, yet only one is actually hired. Separate yourself with a great story.

Write in 1st person, it's your resume right? It's not a playbill or an obituary. Include things outside of what you've done; visitors can visit read on if they want to see what you've done. Tell them why you've done what you have done so far, and how you did it.

Leave Out the Fluff

Just like in your headline, leave out the buzzwords that don't offer any insight into you as a professional. DO include those keywords you found while researching top user profiles, as the repetitive inclusion of these keywords is crucial in optimizing your profile.

Attention span is now at an all time low, and will continue to decrease. People are constantly distracted and their attention is fleeting – there is no need to use all of the available 2000 characters. The expression "less is more" applies here. Entice people to want to learn more about you, without saying you need to learn more about me.

Call to Action

Most users don't include a call to action in their profile summary. Intentionally or unintentionally, visitors come across your profile. Once they land on your profile, you have control over what action they take next.

Just like a captivating blog post or sales letter, you must include an action for readers to take. With LinkedIn, connecting with other users is the most rewarding action. By connecting with others, you are capturing this person's attention for a lifetime and not just those 15 seconds they are on your profile. Every time you submit a new feed update or share a business opportunity, their attention will be captured again as your update appears in their feed.

Whether you are searching for a job, or looking to find a business partner, your call to action should be the same – it should be to connect.

Users on LinkedIn will not be comfortable with any other call to action. Getting profile visitors to leave LinkedIn, visit your website, or pick up the phone proves a difficult challenge and will deter more visitors than attract.

Instead, leave a quick blurb such as:

"As a search engine marketing professional in the New York area, I value building a network with talented individuals who are passionate about digital marketing, building websites, and testing new business ideas online. If you value these same things, send me an Invitation to connect ".

This tells visitors exactly what to expect if they connect with you. By connecting, they will get to see your feed updates, join in discussion, and become 2nd connections to your 1st connections, so tell them what to expect.

7. Experience

Here is where you will input your current work position, as well as past positions. Mirroring the experience section of your resume, inputting your work experience is very straightforward.

Company Name
This is where you will input the company's name. If your company has a LinkedIn Company Page, it will populate as a choice once you begin typing the name in. Otherwise, you can enter the company name in manually.

Title

This is where you will enter in your role with the company – such as Account Manager of Sales. Remember, we left this out of our Headline in an effort to include keywords and attract industry professionals, so it's important that we clarify the exact role in this section. Some titles can be unclear or ambiguous, so consider further explaining your role or using a more common titling.

Location
While we've chosen a wider geographical location for our current location in the headline, here we need to specify exactly where each position is/was located.

Time Period
Simply enter the dates in which you've held your previous positions. Check the "I currently work here" box if it's the position in which you are currently at.

Description
This is where you will enter what the role entailed. Take your time filling out this section. It's best that you draft your job descriptions in a word processer such as Microsoft Word. The text editor within the description box does not allow for easy use of bullet points and other simple features.

Using Word, you can include bullet points to help create a more attractive and succinct list of your roles, achievements, and experiences gained. Once again, make sure to include the keywords that you've targeted and inputted in your headline and summary.

You should look to include all past positions in this section, but only positions that validate and emphasize what you've stated in your summary. Inserting past job experiences with no relation to your current undertakings will only detract attention away from your professional intentions. It's better to leave off unrelated experience, than to confuse visitors.

8. Upload A File or Add A Link

You can enhance your profile summary, experience, and education sections by attaching helpful links and media. LinkedIn's new update allows users to upload media and insert links, helping users craft a comprehensive experience for their profile visitors. This feature is different than the Additional Recommended Sections just mentioned earlier. Those are stand-alone components that can be added to your profile.

In regards to media, LinkedIn allows only certain file types to be shared. They have a list of approved partner sites for which you can choose from. Popular choices include sharing presentation slides from Slideshare, videos from Youtube, or audio recordings from Sound Cloud.

This is a very new feature. A complete list of approved content providers can be found here:
http://help.LinkedIn.com/app/answers/detail/a_id/34327

It's best practice to only include relevant content or links in these sections. Unless you are a recent graduate, it does not make sense to include media from your senior semester project. However, if you recently presented a keynote address at a huge industry conference and it's been recorded in audio/video format, then you should certainly add this to your summary section.

For your experience section, you are allowed to include media for each position you held. This is a great way to show what you've done, rather than talk about what you've done. If you were part of a successful 3-month international business development project, include a SlideShare presentation from that project within that job description.

Pro-Tip: Add Your Website
In regards to links, you include a link to your own website or portfolio. Take advantage of link inclusion by adding any of

your own links, websites, and services you offer. This opportunity is somewhat surprising because it allows you to direct visitors to leave LinkedIn, something LinkedIn doesn't benefit from. Those that use links properly to complement their profiles should be able to gain additional traffic to their websites and offsite content.

9. Skills & Expertise

Skill sections use to be static, allowing you to only list your skills. It was very easy to manipulate and boast of the many skills one had (or so they said). While exaggerating here didn't help one build an honest profile or valuable network, search results did become flooded with "overqualified" users due to all the keywords stuffed in to the skill section. Those savvy enough to take advantage of this section could outrank other users who were truly more qualified.

Now, due to another update from LinkedIn, the skills you list are not only visible to your network, but they can be endorsed by your 1st degree connections. For example, if you list Social Media Management as a skill, any of your 1st degree connections can now vouch for you having that skill and "endorse" it. A thumbnail of their picture will appear next to that skill, and visitors can see a total count of how many people endorsed that skill.

This somewhat trivial update has caused big implications in terms of networking, mostly for the better. We will discuss these implications as we explore the etiquette of giving/receiving skill endorsements in the next chapter.

Users can list up to 50 skills in their skill section. Click the edit button in the skill section to add a new skill. Just start typing in your desired skill and LinkedIn will start to auto populate suggestions. Find the skill you wish to include, and then just hit add.

Again, this is another place where specificity is crucial. If you list "marketing" as a skill, no visitor will understand what that means – are you a good marketer for law firms? Are you a good marketer in regards to print media? The more specific you are, the more helpful you make your profile to visitors looking to gain more information about you.

10. Education

This section is easy to complete; it's where you list any schools you've attended. There are options for including descriptions and listing activities, but for most professionals, you need only list the name of the school, the degree, field of study, and date range for your studies. Additional information should be included if it includes a really prestigious award, grant, project, or something that still holds value today.

As for recent graduates, with a more bare profile, this is a good section to include achievements, class projects, and other information that can help paint a picture to employers. For those amidst pursuing a degree, you can include the expected date of graduation.

Pro Tip – Including Links & Media

This is one of the sections where you are allowed to include media and links. Did you speak as the valedictorian at your graduation? Include the video clip here. Maybe you just finished a yearlong project for your MBA – include a SlideShare presentation here. Don't just stick in a favorite essay of yours from your sophomore year in college.

11. Additional Info – Interests, Personal Details, Advice For Contacting You

This is where you can include some additional information that doesn't appropriately fit elsewhere.

Interests

This a great place to add tons of keywords that you've already included in your profile headline, summary, and experience sections. This section doesn't read like a summary, it's just a list of all interests. Separate your interests with commas and then click save.

Once you add interests, you or your visitors can actually click on each of the interests and be taken to a search results page that lists all users that have the same keyword listed somewhere in their profile. You may find other great keywords used in these users' profiles, giving you more suggestions to include in your profile.

Personal Details
You can add your birthdate and marital status here. There is no reason to include this information, as this is the "professional" network. Some employers may be interested in hiring either younger or older, so this could work against you.

If you list this information, you can click the lock icon next to both your birthdate and martial status to select who can see this information – your connections, network, everyone, or just you.

Advice For Contacting You
You can copy and paste the same "call to action" placed in your profile summary into this section. In addition to asking visitors to connect with you, you can include an email or phone number if you wish to provide visitors with a more direct communication method.

12. Recommendations

While skill recommendations have become all the craze, traditional recommendations still carry much more weight and should be high priority when building your profile. During the interview process for most positions, candidates are asked to provide letters of recommendation, with 3 recommendations being a sufficient number to pass on to the interviewer.

Although there is no limit on the amount of recommendations one can have, the quality of your recommendations is more important than the quantity of recommendations. A personalized, thorough recommendation written by a manager/thought leader in your company carries a lot more value than all of your skill recommendations combined.

While you can get your friends to write such recommendations, they won't carry any value. Your friends are most likely in a different industry, with a different company, and are at an equivalent experience level – and their profile will illustrate that.

You want stellar recommendations from those people who will continue to elevate their careers within your industry. As they progress in their careers, their recommendation will become more valuable as well.

We will discuss the art of giving/receiving these recommendations in the next chapter – just know that you can opt to display/not display any recommendations. Many people get worried that past employers may try to tarnish their profile with a negative recommendation – luckily your safeguarded by LinkedIn's options.

All of the recommendations you wish to be displayed will be listed in this section. To manage all of you're received and given recommendations, you can access your recommendation manager here: https://www.LinkedIn.com/references

13, 14, & 15. Connections, Groups, and Following

Positioned at the bottom of your profile, these 3 sections act as good reference for organizing one's connections, groups, and followers. This is one area where you can't brag or boast, but visitors will still find value by browsing these 3 sections. Visitors will get a better understanding of your network, and what subjects truly interest you. These sections help paint a bigger picture about you to your network and potential connections.

When recruiting, if I come across a GREAT candidate with a GREAT profile, I will scour their connections, groups, and news sources to find other GREAT candidates. This is why it's crucial to create a network full of other talented professionals. Your perceived talent is heightened when you surround yourself with other highly talented individuals.

Connections
Your connections will be listed here. As already discussed in the settings section, you have the option of allowing connections to view your other connections.

Groups
The groups you are a member of are listed here. Private groups are hidden on your profile, unless the person viewing your profile is also a member of the group.

Following
As discussed earlier, you can follow Companies, Influencers, and Channels (News). This section of your profile just lists these various followings, making it easy for visitors to see what interests you.

Rearranging Your Profile's Layout

LinkedIn permits users to rearrange the order of all the profile sections we've just discussed. When you enter "edit profile" mode, you will find a two-way arrow icon appended to each section of your profile. You can click and drag entire profile components to rearrange the order of the information displayed.

It's best practice to leave your profile summary at the top of your profile. You want this to be one of the first thing visitors see listed when coming across your profile. Since most users are used to the default configuration, rearrangement of sections should only be considered for moving certain sections closer to the top. You may want to include one of the new add-on sections closer to the top of your profile, such as the projects component where you can display portfolio work.

With the new content rollout by LinkedIn, links and media are now allowed within the profile summary. That being the case, it may make sense to just supplement your summary with these inclusions, rather than rearranging sections.

Public Profile

We are almost ready to go out and create a network that will provide us with tons of career opportunities. Before we get to it, let's look at the last aspect of editing our profiles - our "Public Profile". With our profiles now complete, we need to address what information is/isn't publically displayed. Adjusting our public profile is different than the settings discussed in the last chapter.

Public profile settings allow you to control the information that appears when people using search engines come across your profile. For example, anybody that is searching for your name in Google and comes across your profile will only be shown what you dictate here.

To edit your public profile settings, head to the top of your profile where the grey "Edit Profile" button is located. Click the drop down arrow to display more options – at which point you will find and click "Manage Public Profile Settings". You will be taken to a settings page and to the right of your profile, this box of options will appear:

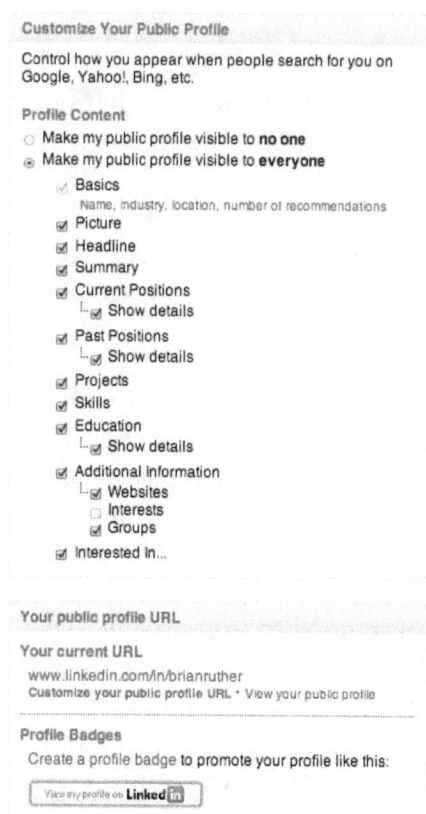

Customize Your Public Profile

This section allows you to make your public profile either
available to no one, or everyone. Since we've built an accurate
depiction of our professional life, it's suggested that we make
our public profiles visible to everyone. Unless you are
extremely keen and tactful about protecting your information
from the public, Google probably already reveals many things
about you already. You might as well allow your career to
benefit from such transparency, as we've crafted our ideal
profile.

You will find the many components of your profile listed here;
you can check/uncheck any component to display publicly.
Again, it's best to allow this information to be displayed, but
you may decide there are a few things that you wish to leave

out. Maybe past education or past positions do a poor job at explaining your career direction, in which case you can deselect them.

Public Profile URL

This setting allows you to change the default URL of your public profile's webpage. A small optimization of your pubic profile URL provides immense benefit in terms of increased visibility in the result pages of search engines. Additionally, this same tweak to your public profile URL will help you enhance your personal brand.

Instead of your Public Profile URL being:

http://www.LinkedIn.com/pub/John-Doe/18/a32/2be

You can change it to read:

http://www.LinkedIn.com/in/johndoe

Why is this important? You are probably not the only one with your name, and another "you" may come up first in the search results of Google or LinkedIn. While we'll spare you the horror stories of misguided search results (employers mistaking candidates for criminals with the same name), it's important that you establish your personal brand on the web. When someone types in "your name", you want to have control over the profiles, websites, and the information that shows up.

By changing the public profile URL, search engines are better informed as to what this URL links to. When you have a bunch of random numbers and letters in your URL, it's misleading to the search engines and visitors as well.

Click the "Customize Public Profile" URL tab and a pop up box will appear. Here you can enter in your entire name with no hyphens or spaces. If your name is already taken, the next best thing is to just add a number after your name. Don't put in a middle name or anything that may mislead the search engines.

So if www.LinkedIn.com/in/yourname is taken, than your next best option is www.LinkedIn.com/in/yourname1

Badges

LinkedIn supplies pre-built "badges" that hyperlink to your profile. If you have a blog, website, or email signature where you can place a badge icon – click on the "create a badge" link and you will be directed to a page with several badge options. Find the badge you wish to use and copy the html code in the text box to the right. You can then paste this code wherever you desire the badge to appear.

With our profiles built and optimized for both visitors and search engines, it's time to build our influential network!

Part Five: The Guide To Networking Like A Pro & Building An Extremely Valuable Network

A brilliantly crafted LinkedIn profile is only as valuable as the network viewing it. You may have 500+ connections on LinkedIn, but if you provide no value to those users and visa versa, your network is worthless. While one may think a larger network is more beneficial than a smaller network, this is not the case.

Your network on LinkedIn should mirror that of your network in real life. In addition to connecting with those already in your "real" network, LinkedIn gives you the leverage to grow your network much more quickly, and interact with users you may have never been exposed to otherwise.

While many tools are in place to help you expand your network, it doesn't mean you should go on a networking binge by adding everyone to your network. It's more beneficial that you create a highly collaborative network that provides extensive value indefinitely, than to build a massive, unfamiliar network fostered by little connectivity and helpfulness.

You may be thinking that there's no downside to just going out and building a massive network...and for the most part, it's not extremely harmful. However, by doing so, it makes it much harder to extract value from your network. When you log in to your LinkedIn account, you want everything to be tailored as to enhance your networking experience. The information appearing in your home update feed should always be helpful, giving you insight into what your connections are doing, relevant industry news, and opportunities geared towards your career path. When you build your network with only growth in mind, this tailored experience will diminish.

If you connect with users whose careers will never intersect with yours or with users whom you've never actually interacted with, allowing them inside your network won't change that. These loose connections will then start to hinder your experience.

For example, one of these hardly known connections may be using you to get in contact with other users in your network – messaging and bothering your truly valuable connections and mentioning your name to do so. Additionally, their feed updates will appear in your home feed, clogging your home feed and diluting content and information shared by your valuable 1st connections.

It's important that we grasp this distinction between a massive network and a valuable network. Of course, you can have a massive network that is also valuable – there is no downside to such a network. We just want to avoid building a massive network for the sake of building a massive network.

Your former co-worker with just 70 connections most likely landed his/her amazing new job offer through intensive networking done by communicating in groups and reaching out directly to top level hiring managers, whereas a similar coworker with the same intent of finding a new position has been growing his/her network to 500+ connections only to have no such "luck".

The ultimate goal of this chapter is for you to build an incredibly powerful network, regardless of size, that provides you with an outlet for simultaneously providing value to your connections and seizing the value they provide.

In building your network, the connectivity structure now comes in to play. In the first chapter, we explored the different levels of connection. Now, we must understand what exactly each connectivity level implies for networking purposes.

Here's A Quick Refresher:

LinkedIn users are classified as either inside or outside of your network. Users inside of your network are denoted by a certain degree of connection.

1st Degree Connections – These are the people you are directly connected with. You will see a symbol next to their name stating they are a 1st degree connection.

2nd Degree Connections – These are the people that are directly connected with one of your 1st degree connections. You will see a symbol next to their name stating they are a 2nd degree connection.

3rd Degree Connections – These are the people that are directly connected with one of your 2nd degree connections. You will see a symbol next to their name stating they are a 3rd degree connection.

Outside of these three major connection levels, there's an additional way for users to be considered inside of your network. If you are a member of a Group, all other group members will be considered part of your network. You will see a symbol next to their name indicating they are a Group connection. If you are also a 1st degree connection with such a group member, that connection will take precedence and they will be listed as a 1st degree connection.

Members that do not fall within any of these connection classifications will be considered outside of your network. There will be a small notification next to their name that displays "Out of your network".

Establishing Your First "1st Degree" Connections

The most powerful way to start making 1st Degree connections is simply to build a great profile. By doing so, all of your friends, colleagues, and business associates will be able to find your profile by completing a search on LinkedIn or Google, and invite you to connect. Take time going through the last chapter, and ensure you've optimized your profile.

Building a great profile will help you in getting started, but to get things really moving you need to find those in your "real life" network on LinkedIn. By connecting with your colleagues and business associates, these users become 1st Degree connections. These few connections are all you need before LinkedIn starts suggesting other users for you to connect with.

In addition to getting started on your own, LinkedIn will suggest that you leverage contacts from other networks and services you are part of. This includes your email contacts from various email providers; LinkedIn will ask if you want to import your email addresses to help you find your friends/coworkers on LinkedIn.

While this may initially seem annoying or somewhat invasive, it is not! This is a great way to jumpstart your network as you this just speeds up the process of connecting to those who you've already deemed worthy of being in your network.

During these initial prompts by LinkedIn, you will essentially be guided through what is known as the "Invitation" process. You will be sending/receiving invitations with other users; this is the process used to establish 1st Degree connections.

In a somewhat sneaky fashion, LinkedIn will also try to get you to send invitations to all of your contacts that may not have yet registered a profile on LinkedIn. This is where they are pushing their own agenda, getting users to help grow their own platform. While this may seem a little overbearing, you may want to consider sending your contacts requests to join LinkedIn.

Not only will their activity on LinkedIn increase your network's value, but also these users may end up discovering a new career opportunity for which you will receive the credit. However, due to the popularity of the platform, odds are you won't find many of your contacts not yet registered on LinkedIn.

You've Established Your First Batch Of Connections
So, with your profile setup and a few invitations sent out thanks to LinkedIn's invitation prompts, you start to see a few notifications that your invitees have accepted your invitation and have become 1st Degree connections.

It's important that you establish a very selective, initial batch of first connections. These connections will provide you the framework for your which your network will grow from. By establishing 1st Degree connections, the number of users now considered "In Your Network" grows exponentially. You may only have 20 1st Degree connections at this point, but your "in network" connections may consist of thousands of members. This is because the connections of your first 20 connections are considered to be a part of your network.

Finding Users To Connect With To Enhance Your Network's Value

Again, just as in "real life", you won't have to venture too far away from your already established network to find other users to connect with. If you are a graphic designer who's client base is mostly musicians and artists, connect with these clients on LinkedIn. By doing so, you will now become 2nd Degree connections with many other musicians and artist who may be interested in your work.

LinkedIn shouldn't be viewed as an overwhelming platform, one where several hours must be spent interacting with others every day. LinkedIn is simply a tool for leveraging your already established network to broaden your connections, helping you connect with users adjacent to your network in which mutually benefit is tangible.

To find such users where mutual benefit and value is interchanged, we must look to the fringe of our networks. This is where we will find users with shared connections, professional goals, or both.

To find these users, there are three optimal methods:
- Via connections of our connections
- Using advanced search
- Groups

Connections Of Our Connections
The first place we should look is through the connections of our 1st Degree Connections. By visiting the profile of any of our 1st Degree connections, we can scroll to the bottom to find a listing of their connections. Some users may have disabled their connections component from being visible in which case you won't be able to see these connections, but this is rare.

This strategy alone will give you access to a massive database of 2nd Degree connections. Since these users are already within your network, expect to share more than just this mutual connection – including additional connections, interests, skills, work experience, and group membership. The connections of your connections represent some of the best users to become 1st Degree connections with and reaching out to them won't feel like pulling teeth.

Advanced Search
We've taken a look at LinkedIn's search capabilities, but have to see them in actin. LinkedIn's advanced search capabilities are extremely powerful in delivering highly relevant results. Using just the search bar, we can quickly pull up any of our connections as LinkedIn will start delivering results in the underneath dropdown.

There will be times when we connect with others at a networking event (real life), but forgot to exchange contact information. This is where using the advanced search capabilities found within the search results page becomes particularly useful.
To perform a user search, simply enter in the name of the user or keyword such as "graphic designer" into the search box. LinkedIn will return a results page that includes all types of results with your keywords in it, this includes: People, Jobs, Companies, Groups, Updates, and messages from your Inbox. We now have to narrow our results using filters so only user results are returned. In the left sidebar, you must select "people" so that only users now appear in your search results.

Let's say you only remember the first name of a person you've just met at a business conference. You can just start by inputting their name - lets call this person Gabriel. Just using this name, LinkedIn returns 270,000 results where the word Gabriel is somewhere to be found. We now have to narrow our results using filters so that only users are returned. On the left hand side you select "people" so that only users now appear in your search results.

With "people" selected, new filters will appear to help you narrow your search further. These filters include: Relationship, Location, Current Company, Industry, Past Company, School, and profile Language.

Odds are, you will remember something else about this person, whether it be their company, location, or schooling. Furthermore, if this person you've met was at an industry conference, there's a good chance that this person will already be "in your network" as a 2nd or 3rd connection. Using the relationship filter, you can quickly look at all of the "Gabriels" in your network, which will usually return a successful match.

If the relationship filter doesn't return a match, we can look at using the advanced search fields. Click on the "Advanced" link at the top of the left sidebar. New search fields will appear, and additional criteria you may know about this person can be entered. All of the search filters will also be included here so you can command an exact search. Get comfortable using advanced search filters and you will have no problem finding anybody or anything within LinkedIn's platform.

Groups
Later in this chapter we explore leveraging groups for expanding our networks, but it's important to note that groups offer the best, most informal way to network with users of shared professions, skillsets, interests, and business intentions. Once you join a group, you can send messages directly to other group members as well as invitations to connect, depending on their account settings.

We now have identified users that will enrich our networking experience – it's time to connect with them.

How To Connect With Users

Now that we've discovered where to find highly relevant users to connect with, we must actually add them as 1st Degree connections. Directly connecting with other users, and thus establishing a 1st Degree connection, can only be done so through acceptance of an "Invitation".

Invitations are similar to a "friend request" on Facebook. By either accepting an invitation sent to you, or by a user accepting your invitation, a 1st Degree connection is established. You will now be able to freely communicate with your new connection and take advantage of all features/settings only made available to users of 1st degree connectivity.

This includes messaging, viewing all information listed on their profiles, getting introduced to their first connections (now your 2nd connections), and seeing updates from/about them in your news feed.

However, you cannot send an invitation to connect with anyone you please. LinkedIn has implemented several stipulations for sending/receiving Invitations as a safe guard against spammers and those looking to abuse the power of LinkedIn's affluent and robust network.

Depending on your current level of connection with the user you intend on connecting with, and their settings, there are 3 ways in which you can go about connecting.

First, you most likely will be able to directly send an **Invitation** to such user. If this isn't possible due to their settings, you will have to use either the **Introductions** feature or send an **InMail** to establish communication. This may seem a little confusing, but you will appreciate these connectivity prohibitions as they protect you from unwarranted requests to connect.

It's important to note that LinkedIn continues to change the settings/permissions of connecting with others. The following information is currently applicable, but may become outdated – stay tuned for notifications of when updates to this book are made available – free lifetime downloads are available for the kindle edition of this book.

Sending & Receiving Invitations

The most common way to connect with another user is through directly sending an invitation. You may have unknowingly used the invitation feature when establishing your first few connections. Sending and receiving invitations is the primary way we will build our networks, and will most likely be the only method needed to do so.

Invitation Etiquette
LinkedIn highly recommends that you only send invitations to those users you already know. If you attempt to connect with somebody that you don't know and that person makes note that your invitation is unwarranted, LinkedIn may ban your account.

Aside from banding your account, they may adjust your account to make it tougher to connect with others. This is a huge pain, so it's suggested that you add a personal message to each of your invitations, even if you know the person quite well.

Adding this personal message is additionally beneficial in a networking sense. It will remind those people you may have just brushed shoulders with who you are and why you should become connections. Face it, sometimes you may not remember every face or name of those you meet out, especially when many networking events include an open bar.

Who Can You Send Invitations To?
In a very recent update, LinkedIn now allows you to send Invitations to any user, unless the user has changed this default setting. While this greatly reduces the once imposed barriers of connecting with others, it's very important not to abuse this freedom. As mentioned above, LinkedIn can easily repeal this freedom if you abuse it.

This shouldn't be a problem for any reader of this book, as we've thoroughly explained the value in building a highly personalized network and not just a vast, unengaged network.

The only users that you won't be able to send an invitation to are those who've adjusted their settings. They've chosen to only accept invitations from people that know their email address, or whom they've placed in their "Imported Contacts" list. These imported contacts were populated from their email accounts, so if you don't know the person's email you won't be able send them an Invite.

Who Can Send You An Invitation?

By default, your account will be open to all invitations unless you alter this setting. In the Settings chapter, we looked at this default setting, which can be found in the communications tab. By default, your setting for receiving invitations will be set to: "Anyone on LinkedIn (Recommended)"

Ideally, you should leave this setting as is – unless you are a very well known executive, industry leader, or person with very in demand skills who can't be bothered. For example, a very talented computer programmer may receive 15 Invitations to connect every day because programming is a highly desired skill.

If this is you, those truly looking to connect or that hold a real career opportunity for you will make the effort to get in touch either using a paid feature like an InMail or find you through another communication channel. Trust me on this, as I will go to the end of the earth to connect with such highly sought after candidates. Use your judgment here, you know best if you are to benefit/lose out from this extra openness.

If you decide to limit invitations, you can choose to only receive invitations from users that know your email (the one used as your primary email for your account) or those whom you've directly imported as potential contacts from your email accounts and are part of you "imported contacts" list.

Sending An Invitation

After finding a user you wish to connect with using the strategies discussed earlier, venture to their profile page. In their profile header, you should find a button labeled "Connect". Clicking this will take you to the invitation page. Again, some users will have opted out of the open invitations settings in which the "Connect" button will not be available.

Pro-Tip: Alternative Way To Connect

You may not be shown the "Connect" button directly on another's users profile due to LinkedIn's constant feature updates and alterations. Try finding the user via search so they appear as a small thumbnail in the search results. Next to their name and headline, the "connect" button may appear.

The Invitation Page

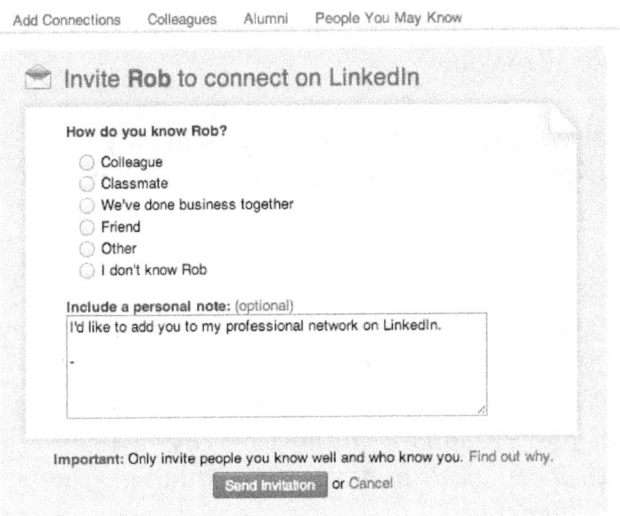

You will be first asked to select how you know the other user. The first four selections (colleague, classmate, we've done business together, and friend) are the best selections because

LinkedIn will not require that you know the person's email address in order to send the invitation.

If this user is/was a colleague, classmate, or business partner, you will be asked to select the company, school, or business that you share with this person. Since we have already set up our profiles, all of these possible choices will be populated for you – all you need to do is select the shared company, school, or business. If it's not listed, you can enter it in manually.

If the first four options do not apply, you are left with "Other" and "I don't know this person". These options will require you knowing the email address of the user.

Pro Tip – Say Your Just A Friend
Be their friend! If it seems the only options that apply are the last two, and you don't have their email address, select the "Friend" option. Even if you wouldn't call this user a friend, and would never "Facebook" them – this is the most seamless and harmless way to send an invitation. Be careful when doing this as the recipient may mark your invite as spam in which LinkedIn could penalize you.

However, we've already discussed that we should only be connecting with users of whom we've connected with in "real life".

Adding A Personal Note
It's always beneficial adding a personal note to your invitation request, especially if the user was met in passing at a networking event. You only have 250 characters (about 40 words) to explain your reason for connecting. Give a direct reason for them to accept your invitation by explaining the benefits of being connected.

Most likely you will have a reason to input, such as a mutually shared career or business benefit. For a more general invitation request, such as an alumnus you faintly knew, your benefit can be more general.

For Example:

Hi Brian,

As fellow University of Miami alumnus, with a career focus in digital marketing, it would be great to connect as both of our LinkedIn networks would benefit from new connection possibilities and the sharing of relevant content.

Best,
John

Once you've selected your reason for connecting and have added a personal note, send away. The recipient will either accept or ignore your invitation request. If they accept, you will become 1st degree connections, otherwise you will remain connected at the level you previously were.

Receiving Invitations

Based upon your account settings, you will receive an email notification whenever a user looks to connect with you. Their invitation will fall in to your LinkedIn Inbox as well, where you can then decide whether or not to accept their invitation.

Two tabs categorize your inbox: Messages and Invitations.

Head to the invitations tab to see pending invitation requests. Hopefully these requests include personal notes, especially if you are unfamiliar with the user requesting to connect. Beyond the personal note, you will now be able to visit and view their complete profile, which should help you grasp their intentions behind connecting, if they were otherwise unclear.

Once you've investigated the requester, you will have the following options:

1. Accept – They become a 1st degree connection.

2. Reply – You can send a message without accepting the invitation yet.

3. Ignore – This will move the invite into an archived folder. The user won't know that you've ignored their request, and may try to connect again.

4. Report as spam – If the request is unwarranted, too salesy, or malicious – you can submit as spam. This will help LinkedIn penalize or remove this users account.

5. I don't know this person – This appears after you've selected the ignore option. By selecting this option, this will inform Linked that the user may be using LinkedIn inappropriately and they will further monitor this user.

While these are your options, it's very important to note that those receiving your invitations will have the same options. That is why it's very important that you are smart with whom you decide to send an invitation to and that you leverage personal notes to better explain your intentions behind connecting.

If you've found a user, but sending an invitation is restricted, it's time to look at two other routes for connecting: Introductions and InMails.

Introductions

If an invitation is not possible, you must next look to see if an "Introduction" is. Introductions allow you to connect with users in your extended network by getting help from your connections. Let's say you want to connect with a person whose a 2nd or 3rd degree connection, but an invitation won't work. You must find and message a connection of yours who is connected with this user.

You will be requesting an introduction from this user. You will draft a message that this person can pass along to the intended user, at which point you may wish to ask to connect.

If your connection is willing to help, your connection can either decide to pass your message along to the intended person (if the intended recipient is a 2nd Degree connection) or pass your message to another shared connection who then decides to forward your message or not (if the recipient is a 3rd Degree connection).

This is kind of confusing, but just know that the further you are away from the intended recipient, the more favors you will be asking your network for. The basic/free account currently includes 5 introductions total (not monthly), and you will be reimbursed an introduction if they are not responded to within 6 months. Premium subscription levels include more invitations.

If and when the intended recipient accepts your introduction, you can then exchange information. At this point, you can will extend/receive an invitation.

How Do I Connect Through Use Of An Introduction
If you have determined that an introduction is the best way to establish communication with another user, here is how you will do it.

First, navigate to this user's profile and click the "Get introduced through a connection" button located in the profile header where the "Connect" button would be. If one person is eligible to establish the introduction, an Introduction Request option will appear where you can click the "Get Introduced" button.

If there are several of your connections that can make the introduction, you can select the connection you wish to introduce you and then click the "Get Introduced" button.

Next, you must draft the message. This message is first going to your connection, not the end user. If your connection decides to approve your introduction, they will forward your message to the intended recipient and will add their own message. With this in mind, you will want to create a message that appeals to your connection, but also takes into consideration that the end recipient will see it. Last, click the send request button.

InMails

For all other LinkedIn users whom you cannot reach via an invitation or introduction, you can use an InMail. InMails are a premium feature and only come with an upgraded account or they can be purchased for $10/per InMail.

For most users, and non-active job seekers, InMails are completely unnecessary. They are intended for bypassing the natural networking methods and features of LinkedIn, and this comes at a cost. While LinkedIn certainly doesn't mind you paying them for this somewhat intrusive feature, many recipients of your InMails will. InMails are sent directly to users, usually notifying them by email if they've changed their settings. While InMails are one of the best tools a recruiter has in his/her toolbox, most users should avoid such forced outreach.

There are exceptions to using InMails. If you are a job seeker, you should certainly be InMailing individuals in organizations for which you seek employment and may have a say in hiring process. This will include HR representatives and recruiters who are use to such outreach, and also those persons currently working in the actual position you seek as you can learn more about the job. Aside from job seekers, recruiters, and direct salespersons, InMails should be used sparingly and very intentionally.

How To Send An InMail

If the person you wish to connect with cannot be contacted via the first two methods, then you will be looking for the "Send InMail" button. This button is also listed in the profile header where the "Connect" button would be.

You now will craft your message as according to your intention for reaching out. It's important to note that InMails receive a guaranteed response as stated by LinkedIn. This does not mean that every recipient will respond, but that LinkedIn will reimburse InMails not responded to. This guaranteed response expires after 7-days, at which point you will be credited back your InMail. LinkedIn "guarantees" a response more as a marketing ploy, but they normally do trigger a response. This occurs because InMails are directed to the recipients email inbox by default.

InMails are usually end up in the email inbox of the recipient and this is very important to note because many users will register their LinkedIn account with their work email. InMails start flooding these users' work email and are ignored because users fear that their employer may discover the conversation. This is why you should stay away from sending InMails if possible. It may come across as invasive and pushy to those foreign to the concept.

Pro-Tip: Bypassing Invitations Requests
When you join a group, you can freely message and connect with fellow group members. We will be looking at Groups more closely, but it's important that tip was included in this section. If a user you wish to connect with chooses to display their groups on their public profile, you can then find and join one of their groups. Once you are a member, you can freely message this person (saving you a $10 InMail purchase if that was your last resort).

How To Engage With Your Network

Now that we've exhausted the ways to get invitations in front of fellow LinkedIn members, and are building networks full of value in an efficient, safe manner, its time to actually interact with our networks.

Updates

Your feed updates are an excellent way to share value amongst your network. Unlike Facebook and Twitter, updates should only be shared sparingly, and should not be used as commentary on your personal and even professional endeavors.

Where Do Your Updates Go?

Your updates will be shared across all of your 1st Degree Connection's homepage streams. If what you've shared is liked, commented on, and/or shared, your update will be given more weight by LinkedIn and will have a "stickier" effect. LinkedIn will keep the posting atop the home feeds of your connections, making sure it is seen by your connections. If your network engages extensively with your update, LinkedIn may even include it in weekly digest emails. These weekly round up emails are sent directly to users' emails and include important happenings within the users' network.

With every update you submit, your goal should be to share something so riveting that it can reach this level. The exposure of having LinkedIn promote your updates via email is priceless. Your network will increasingly see you as an authority, one who's content is so important that LinkedIn has decided to share it.

What Can You Share?

You are allowed to share updates up to a 600 characters limit. In addition to text, updates can include links and attachments. Images, documents, and presentations can be uploaded directly in your updates box; this can be done by clicking the paperclip attachment icon.

When you paste a link into your update box, LinkedIn will analyze the link and extract a relevant description and picture from the intended link destination. You can leave this extra information in your update posting, or remove it by pressing the little "x" icon.

A recent update now allows you to "mention" other users in your status update. Similar to Twitter, start by typing the @ symbol. Next, start typing the user's name you wish to include and you will find a dropdown of matching results. You can even mention companies who have a LinkedIn Company Page. Those tagged in your updates will receive notification. This is a great way to involve your company in your update, helping increase exposure of the Company Page. Also, it's great for sharing highly targeted content with those users who will benefit from it the most.

Who Sees What?
After you've constructed your update, you can select to whom it's shared with. There are 3 options as to who you will make this update "visible to" using the dropdown menu near the share box: LinkedIn, LinkedIn & Your Twitter Following, and Your Connections.

If visibility is set to "LinkedIn", your update could appear on:
- Your 1st-degree connections' homepages
- Your 2nd or 3rd degree connections' homepages if commented upon, liked, or re-shared
- Your Profile page's activity feed

If visibility is set to "Your connections", your update may appear:
- Your 1st-degree connections' homepages
- Your Profile page's activity feed

If set to Connections & Twitter (You must first connect your Twitter to your LinkedIn in your account settings)
- Your 1st-degree connections' homepages
- Your Profile page's activity feed
- And then LinkedIn will also Tweet your message

The Do's And Don'ts Of Status Updates

There are several do's and don'ts of status updates. Ultimately, you want to share things that add immense value to your network. Keep your focus on providing as much value as possible to help your connections in their professional journey.

Do Share:

Industry Insights

Odds are, any industry insight that you have found helpful and applicable in your career, will also be found as helpful and applicable to your network (assuming you've built a highly relevant network).

By sharing content-rich, professional insights, you become a more valuable asset within your connection's network. If you are a web designer who's always sharing highly valuable insight on the newest web design technologies and trends, fellow web designers will view you as an industry leader. For those users in your network, but outside of the web design industry, they will begin to associate you with web design and you will become top of mind – which will lead to all sorts of career opportunities.

Case Studies

People love to see success stories, failures, and how they came to be. The more in-depth these findings are (facts, figures, profits), the better.

Events

There may be events that your network could benefit from by attending. In addition to in person events, there may even be virtual webinars or events in which anyone in your network can attend, regardless of geographic location.

Questions

Asking purposeful questions may stir up great discussion in which many connections will add helpful information. This will create a threaded discussion with tons of valuable content – one that people may even bookmark as a reference for future support. Even if you share very little insight, the discussion and information shared will be attributed to you and your profile image will be positioned at the top of the thread.

Don't Share:

Pitches / Sales Copy
Direct selling on LinkedIn is not only frowned upon, but also highly ineffective. There's no quicker way to become distrusted by your network than by trying to sell them your service or product right away. However, if you have an amazing case study or incredibly factually blog post/article that explains the benefits of your service and product, this may be something worth sharing – as you are providing value to your network. In return, they may share your content and unknowingly become a salesperson for you.

Personal Stories
Facebook is where you can share anything your heart desires; LinkedIn is for professional networking – so act professionally. Nobody on LinkedIn will benefit from you sharing pictures of your new puppy, unless they are a dog walker and are looking for business leads.

Additionally, nobody cares about your personal whereabouts. If you are away at a conference and want others in your network to know, maybe consider sharing a summary blog post of the keynote address or an infographic about the event's importance.

Current Work Situation
Along the same lines as sales copy, you should not be directly addressing your network as to what you seek or want from them. If you are a job seeker, don't post a desperate update about you needing work. Use the many messaging and

networking features to connect with those that may be able to help you out.

How Often Should You Share

Unlike other social networks where your connections are comfortable with receiving your hourly and impulsive updates, LinkedIn differs. You should only be sharing updates at a max of one per day, with better results probably being seen with updates every few days (2-3x per week). Also, it makes very little sense to post updates on the weekend, as only a small fraction of users will see it. Look to post midweek, either early in the morning or around lunchtime. This gives your updates a better chance of being seen and shared during commuting and early afternoon times.

Messaging

Messaging is a free to use feature, available to all users wishing to communicate with their connections. You can message your 1st Degree connections, as well as fellow group members who've allowed messaging in their group settings.

Messages are a great way to get in direct contact with somebody whose email you may not have. A notification, unless they've adjusted their settings, will be sent to their email inbox relaying your message. Messaging is a great replacement for your email address book, business cards, etc. This is a great reason for why you should always directly connect with anyone you work with, networked with, or have conducted business with. You will always have a way to get in touch with these people.

If you receive a business card from someone, send him or her an invite on LinkedIn to solidify this free communication channel.

Sending messages is rather easy. Simply visit the profile of the person you wish to message. Once you've found them, the "Message" button can be found in their profile header. Clicking on this button triggers a pop up message box, just as if you are drafting an email. Fill out the subject line, the message, and then press send. It's as easy as that.

Pro-Tip: Messaging Group Members

Remember, in addition to your 1st connections, you can message fellow group members. Search for these users directly, or find complete listings of group members by heading to the "Members" tab within each group's page.

We've now learned how to expand and communicate with our networks. Although we've optimized our profiles, it's now time to get help from our connections in further optimizing our profiles via recommendations.

Recommendations

According to Newton's law, "To every action there is always an equal and opposite reaction". The same applies for LinkedIn. The more you contribute to your network, the more you will receive in return.

In regards to this concept, LinkedIn continues to expand its' features that facilitate giving. New ways for users to share, give, and extract value from their networks are constantly being added. The most familiar transfer of value lays in the giving/receiving of recommendations.

It is common knowledge throughout the HR and recruiting world that the best employees are those that were referred by other employees. Employee referrals are statistically proven to provide better hires that are more productive, stay with the company longer, and are happier in their positions.

Once a person vouches for another person, they put themselves in the spotlight and open to critique. This is the foundation on which giving/receiving recommendations stem from. The minute you recommend somebody else, you are simultaneously making a statement about yourself.

Many users will brag in their own profiles and falsify information in attempt to get a leg up. Giving and receiving dishonest recommendations can be done just as easily, yet recommendations are rarely abused.

How often will you want to write a glowing, personalized recommendation for someone you truly wouldn't recommend? Nobody wants to jeopardize his or her career and livelihood, especially when there is no incentive. By attaching your name to a false recommendation and recommending subpar professionals, you are jeopardizing how others will view your professional judgment. Even by just being connected with such users whom we wouldn't recommend, we are greatly devaluing the value of our network, as users will begin to distrust the people around us.

We must strive to receive strong recommendations from those highly esteemed connections within our network. Three strong recommendations will greatly outweigh ten, thoughtless recommendations. Additionally, we should only seek recommendations from those in a position that we aspire to. If you are a salesperson at your company, you should be seeking the recommendation from your sales manger, regional sales manager, or even countrywide manager (the higher the better). It adds no value to your profile by having recommendations from another sales person with your same experience level, or a manager from the finance department.

Always seek recommendations from those in the position you aspire to!

When a sales manager submits a recommendation about a salesperson in their company, his or her entire network will be notified of this recommendation in their news feed. The salesperson will gain the recognition of higher ups in the company, and from other companies' sales managers whom are connected with this sales manager.

Not only do our profiles benefit from having this actual written recommendation attached, but this broadcast is being sent out across a highly valuable and relevant network. Someone in a higher up and esteemed position is vouching that your skills are worthy of being recommended. Don't waste this valuable opportunity and profile space by getting your buddy to recommend you, unless your buddy is the highly esteemed Sales Manager.

In the same manner as recommendations, LinkedIn now allows users to endorse their connections on a skill-by-skill basis. This requires very little effort, as it does not take much time or personalization, thus these skill endorsements are not nearly as valuable as regular recommendations. We should focus our time on securing the highest quality recommendations before looking at these skill endorsements.

One last note of importance is that recommendations and skill endorsements carry less value if they are reciprocal. That means, just because your client endorsed you for your web design skills doesn't mean you should endorse them for their marketing skills. This looks somewhat shady, and odds are there was only a one-way relationship in terms of value transfer. They may have designed your website in return for your payment, but chances are slim that they hired you for your marketing skills. Viewers of your profile will take notice of these reciprocal recommendations and this will cause more doubt than confidence in your abilities.

In order to receive, you must first give. But whom should you give to? While it would make sense to give a recommendation to those whose recommendation you seek, you should only be giving a recommendation to those who would benefit from a recommendation coming from you. This would include any current and former colleagues that you managed. Next, you could recommend those whose work you've benefited from.

While these recommendations will not help you directly, these recipients will certainly appreciate your endorsement because it provides great value to their profile and may lead to a career opportunity or new client. They may look to reciprocate your generosity in the form of a recommendation, but these recommendations will probably not benefit you nearly as much. Since you have the option to select which recommendations appear on your profile, you can simply opt out of showing their recommendation. Regardless, this person will now feel somewhat indebted to you and their will be some sort of value reciprocation.

Giving Recommendations

To recommend one of your connections, head to their profile. In their profile headline, you will find the "Message" button. Select the arrow tab next to where it says message. You will then find the option to "Recommend" in the dropdown – select this option and you will see a pop up screen where you can select from 4 options as to recommend this person. You can recommend this connection as a colleague, service provider, business partner, or student. This helps brings context to your recommendation, making it more valuable for the receiving user. After selecting one of these options, you'll be taken to the screen where you will write your recommendation:

You will be required to fill out 3 relationship criteria before writing your recommendation: the basis of recommendation, your title at the time, and person's title at the time. LinkedIn will auto populate choices based on the information found in both of your profiles. Select the appropriate relationship information for each of these 3 sections.

After selecting the appropriate relationship criteria, you will have 3,000 characters (~ 300-400 words) to craft your recommendation.

Writing A Strong Recommendation
In order to write a strong recommendation for your connection, you must understand what business or professional goals they have. If they are a web designer that is always looking for new clients, you will want to speak to those talents assuming you've interacted with them in such manner. A generalized recommendation is useless, as those reading it will not learn about the person's skills, character, and professional abilities.

With a specific understanding of their career ambitions, it makes it very easy to speak on behalf of this person. Be as detailed as possible, but very concise. Your recommendation should speak to specific instances, projects, and interactions in a story like manner as this draws readers in. The provided

3000 characters is way too long, keep it to a paragraph or two at the most.

Once you've completed writing your recommendation – submit it. Your connection will be notified and they can accept it to display on their profile. Additionally, they can choose to hide the recommendation from appearing for whatever reason.

Pro-Tip: No Reciprocal Recommendations

Once you've written recommendations, visitors to your profile can see whom you've written recommendations for by selecting the "given" tab with your recommendations component. This reinforces why it's not a great idea to engage in reciprocal recommendations. They provide less value and such tactics can be seen publicly on your profile.

Requesting/Receiving Recommendations

While it's very easy to request a recommendation on LinkedIn, it's best practice to notify the requested recipient beforehand that you would greatly appreciate their recommendation (in person, via email, etc.). This will greatly improve your chances for receiving their personalized recommendation. Requests should be sent to those who you've established a very successful relationship with, as they will be best for writing a recommendation that really speaks to who you are, what you've done, and your merit.

Sending recommendation requests is simple. Head to your profile and click the arrow next to the "Edit Your profile" button. You will find a dropdown option to "Request Recommendation" in which you will be taken to a request form where there are 3 fields to fill out.

The 3 Fields To Fill Out Your Request

1. What do you want to be recommended for?
This is where you will select the position for which you would like the recipient to speak to. This is very important because

you want to ensure that you are getting relevant and sensible recommendations. You don't want to ask your former boss to speak about your performance at your new job!

2. Who do you want to ask?

LinkedIn allows you to add more than 1 connection to receive your recommendations request. Only those looking to take shortcuts in building their network will find this feature helpful – we will not send mass requests, only singular, personalized requests.

You should be drafting a customized message to every connection you wish to receive a recommendation from. Your personalized message will increase the chances that they deliver a recommendation, and one that is truly helpful. A general request at best will result in a general recommendation.

3. Create Your Message

With just ONE recipient chosen, write a very personalized request explaining to this person why their input would greatly enhance your profile and positively impact your career. This message will make them feel special, and that their input is highly desired. Since these requests should ideally be sent to those who have managed your or are in an advanced position on your career track, it should be easy to address why their esteemed recommendation would greatly enhance your professional trajectory.

Other Recommendation Notes

While you can recommend non-1st Degree connections, you will have to connect with this person in order for the recommendation to appear. This is probably not recommended; you should connect with someone first before writing a recommendation. However, it may work in some instances.

You can manage all of your recommendations in one place. This allows you view all of the recommendations you've given and received. This also allows you to edit recommendations you've given, and choose which recommendations you wish to display on your profile.

To visit your recommendations manager visit this link: http://www.LinkedIn.com/recommendations

Skill Endorsements

Once you've given several recommendations and have secured a few glowing recommendations for you own profile, it's time to give some skill endorsements. Selecting those you will endorse should mirror those whom you given personal recommendations to. You can't possibly give a skill recommendation to somebody outside of your department or industry of which you know little about (unless you've collaborated with them on a project).

Again, reciprocity should not be the driving force endorsements behind skill endorsements. Your connections will only gain value from your skill endorsements if you are in a position to speak about their work or skills.

Skill endorsements can only be given to 1st Degree connections. Simply visit your connections' profile and scroll down until you see their list of skills. You can add your endorsement to each listed skill, and also suggest a new skill that they may not have listed themselves. This is a great opportunity to really provide value for users in your network.

Endorsing a connection for a skill they've yet listed or haven't even thought about including is a great way to get on their radar and brighten up their day. You may want to consider using skill recommendations for sucking up to a manager or someone you are seeking a personalized recommendation from!

Receiving Skill Endorsements
Skill endorsements are different than personalized recommendations, as you are not allowed to request skill endorsements from your network. Since requests aren't currently offered with this feature, LinkedIn takes the liberty of suggesting to your network via email notifications and through homepage reminders that they should recommend your skills.

The best way to receive skill endorsements is to give them to those who've you worked with, as they will be able to respond with skill endorsements that speak to the work you've collaborated on.

Group Networking

We've touched on the importance of joining Groups throughout this book, but we've yet to fully examine how groups can be leveraged to empower you and your network. Groups are the most underutilized aspect of LinkedIn, yet they are probably the most impactful on many fronts. Looking for a new client? Interested in exploring a new career? Seeking a talented freelancer to design your website? Promoting your service? Are you hiring?

Participating in Groups is the answer to all of these questions.

Since this entire chapter's focus is on increasing the value of our networks, we are going to look at how to find the best groups for us to join, how to participate in these groups, and the not so obvious benefits associated with being a group member. In the last chapter we will discuss a few additional group tips intended to help users with specific networking intent, such as job seekers and salespersons.

Groups Overview

Groups are the strongest way to strengthen your personal brand and communicate with likeminded professionals. Groups give you an outlet for sharing expertise and provide an excellent forum for communicating in an efficient manner.

Groups are not organized or managed by LinkedIn. LinkedIn users create groups themselves; any user can create a LinkedIn group, thus becoming the group manager.

All groups fall under one of two types: members-only groups and open groups.

The only real difference between these two types is that group members are the only ones that can view members-only groups' discussions, whereas open group discussions can be read anybody searching the web. Open group discussions can also be shared across other social media networks.

You will be able to differentiate the two groups by a small gray padlock icon next to the group's name. Members-only groups will have the lock icon appended. If the group is an open group, you will not find the padlock icon next to the group's name, meaning all LinkedIn members can view group discussions and entire thread discussions can be shared outside of LinkedIn, such as on Facebook or Twitter.

What's Better? Open Groups Or Members-Only Groups
We must be selective when choosing groups to join, as we want to align our group memberships with our networking efforts. If you are a currently employed job seeker, you will not want a "job search" related discussion to be publicly available. If you are just entering into industry discussion, it does not matter whether your input is made public or not.

In many situations, an open group can help broadcast your insight, commentary, and content in other places. The increased visibility and share ability will allow your contributions to extend further, which could lead to new opportunities.

Benefits of Joining Groups
Groups are centralized around industries, skillsets, interests, and professional goals. They are extremely valuable because they are NOT centralized around brands. You may find a Coca Cola Former Alumni group, which is a great way for former Coca Cola employees to network. However, you won't find simply a Coca Cola group dedicated to the products and services of Coca Cola. The closest feature to this is a company page, but company pages offer less interactive and networking capability.

With commercial motives removed, LinkedIn groups have become a very open, genuine environment for connecting, networking, and providing/extracting value in the form of dialogue, job postings, and quality content.

Being a highly active group member is incredibly empowering, regardless of one's intent. Currently, there are over 1.7 million groups; users are limited to joining no more than 50 groups.

Benefits of Joining Groups Include:

Become a thought leader in your industry.
By constantly partaking in dialogue, starting new conversations, and reaching out to group members, you will be seen as a go to person for whatever the subject matter. Group members will visit your profile to learn more you, which will lead to invitations to connect and hopefully business opportunities in the future.

Tailor your content experience.
By joining groups, you will be able to share and receive the most current news and content in your industry. Group settings will allow you to select if and how you want to be notified of new discussions and content.

Generate leads and sales.
After partaking in conversation and becoming a thought leader amongst your groups, new business opportunities may arise. Since you will be joining groups that match up with well with your networking goals, you will naturally be exposed to opportunity that aligns with your professional goals.

Reaping all the benefits of group participation takes some effort and time, which is why it's essential that you only join relevant groups.

Finding The Best Groups To Join
Wading through the 1.7 million groups can be tricky, and there are a lot of groups that may sound promising, but don't actually offer any real value. For example, there are groups centered

solely on job opportunities that boast tens of thousands of members. While initially this may sound enticing, these groups are dead-end groups.

These groups are too generic and attract spammy type users who are either trying to sell job-seeking services or have less than attractive job opportunities. These members will poach you and your time will be wasted. Remember, specificity is key!

If you are a web designer looking for web design work, joining the group "Job Openings, Job Leads and Job Connections!" with over 38,000 members is like trying to find a needle in a haystack.

However, joining the "Web Standards Design + Development" group gives you access to a more targeted membership base, allowing you to message members directly, find job postings, and share your thoughts about web design with members who actually care.

Furthermore, there are many other types of groups to join outside of the direct industry correlation. One of the best types of groups to join are university alumni groups – you will even find alumni groups dedicated to just one school within a university such as the business, music, or medical school (the more targeted, the better).

Localized groups are also worth joining. They could provide more realizable opportunities and access to local networking events. Even if the "NYC Web Design" group only has eighty members in it, you can become a highly active and visible member.

Now that we've established groups worth joining, let's find them.

How To Find These Groups

Advanced Search

The easiest way to find targeted groups is by using the trusted search bar. Start by entering in keywords surrounding the various types of groups you wish to join. Take advantage of your specific, industry knowledge to bypass many of the generic and fruitless groups. A web designer will be acclimated to certain terms more detailed than just "web design" or "graphic design". They may use the terms "front end web design" or "HTML &CSS" to discover more specific groups.

Your results page will include all types of results that include your keyword in it. We must use the search filters in the left sidebar to narrow our results to display only groups. Once we've narrowed our results to just groups, there are additional filters that will appear. These filters include: Relationship, Categories, and Languages.

The relationship filter allows you to narrow results to only display groups of which your connections are members. You can use the filter to separate groups by those in which 1st, 2nd, or 3rd Degree connections are members of.

The category filter allows you to separate group results by those you are already a member of, open groups, and members-only groups. The last filter, Languages, just helps you select groups in your native language.

Via Your Connections

One of the best ways for finding relevant groups is by looking through the groups that your connections are already members of. Just head to your connections' profiles and scroll down to the very bottom to find a list of all the groups they are part of.

Since we've built a highly relevant network, our connections most likely participate in groups that would be of interest to us. Carefully look through these groups, as some won't make sense to join – such as alumni and organizational groups.

Pro-Tip: Group Composition

Each group provides a sneak peak of the composition of its membership. Groups' statistics pages contain information about the demographics of its group members. You can discover how many members are in a group, the level of discussion, the growth of the group, and most importantly – the breakdown of the group members. This breakdown includes stats on the members' seniority levels, titles and positions, industry, and location.

These statistics can help you identify groups whose memberships consist of high-powered professionals. You can visit the statistics page by looking for the "Group Statistics" box on the right hand side of any group's homepage. Do all of this research before joining the group!

Joining The Group

Once we've found highly relevant groups for which our networking efforts won't go unnoticed, it's time to join.

When requesting to join a group, you are either automatically accepted or your request will be deemed pending. A pending request means that the manager of the group has altered the settings so that he/she must manually accept or decline users. It's careful that you read the group rules set forth by the group manager before requesting to join – as many managers will only accept requests based on the group requirements they put in place. This could occupation, industry, and other determinants.

However, most groups will allow you to join automatically. To join a group, simply hit the "join" button next to the group description in your search results. You can also find the join button on the group's page itself. If accepted, you will receive an email confirmation and instantly gain access to the group's member areas. If not accepted immediately, a pending request notification will appear; you will receive notification of acceptance if and when the manager approves your request.

Pro-Tip: Participate Before Joining
If the group is an open-group (no padlock) you can visit the group page and start participating in conversation without joining. However, you will have to join the group to start your own discussion thread. This is a great way to see if this group is highly interactive and worthwhile.

Networking Via Groups
To best leverage groups for networking, it's imperative to understand the features contained within groups.

Group Discussion Wall
The group discussion wall houses all conversations of the group's members. You will be allowed to contribute here by joining an already established conversation, or by starting your own conversation thread.

Members Page
The Members Page contains a searchable database of all group members. This list is a great resource for finding members to connect with. Remember, you don't need to have a 1st Degree connection with fellow groups members to message them.

Jobs & Job Discussions
These two areas contain are where jobs and opportunities are listed. The job board contains only paid job postings of LinkedIn. The job discussions area is less restricted and allows members to post job listings, links, and discussions that are not correlated to paid listings on LinkedIn. Any posts to the job discussions area are automatically removed after 14 days. Group managers have complete control over what is posted in both of these job areas; group settings may allow members to post in either area.

Promotions

This component is one of the least important group features. It contains all promotions that the group manager and members post. These promotions are usually for products/services and many members abuse this area. Most times these promotional posts are quite spammy, go unmonitored, and provide very little value to the group. The group manager can remove any of these posts, and also move promotion type posts from the discussion wall to this section.

Joining The Discussion
Before we start our own discussions, it's important to join already established conversations. You should look for the most popular discussions to join because these threads will receive the most attention and visibility among group members, and non-group members if the group is an open one. By default, LinkedIn lists the most popular discussions at the top of the discussion wall. You can change this sorting for the most recent discussions to be shown instead.

By participating in popular discussions and heated debate, you will gain recognition amongst fellow group members and the group manager. Daily and weekly roundup emails, that include the most popular discussions, are sent directly to group members, unless they've opted out of these notifications. By default, members are signed up to receive these emails and most never change this setting. If you provide valuable information and answers in these highly visible discussions, your input will end up in the inboxes of your fellow group members. If you can successfully maintain valuable discussion, starting your own discussions won't be essential.

Pro-Tip: Introduce Yourself To Others
Many groups contain a discussion thread for welcoming new members, giving new members an outlet for introducing themselves. Aside from oneself and explaining your reason for joining the group, put aside a few minutes every week for welcoming new members. You can "like" or reply to their introductory post and welcome them to the group. These

members will appreciate you reaching out, thus increasing the odds that they will comment and share your future contributions to the group.

Starting Your Own Discussion
You can also choose to start your own discussion, which will be posted to the discussion wall. You are given the options to include a title, message, and a link. Self-promotion of your business, services, or products is highly frowned upon and could get you kicked out of your group depending on the manager's discretion. Other members will mark you as a dishonest, non-helpful member and will ignore any future postings.

Just as a fair warning, most group managers will not allow you to post job discussions or promotion like material on the main discussion wall. They will remove your content, move it the Job and Promotions areas, or discard you from the group.

The best way to sell yourself or business is by contributing value. Post an incredibly insightful comment, question, or link to a blog/article/report that contains valuable insight relevant to members of the group. These types of posts will stir up conversation naturally, and other members will begin to contribute. Over time, these group members will begin to trust your insight and may look to you for professional expertise either in the form of a job offer, partnership, or in becoming a client (whatever your networking intent is).

Additionally, polls can be submitted to the group discussion. This feature can be found by clicking the "Poll" tab within your discussion submission box. You can fill out up to 5 selections, or answers, for your poll. This is a great way to spark conversation and even collect data to help you improve your own services and products.

Pro-Tip: Follow The Rules

Check the Rules Page of each group you join. Make sure your participation is aligned with the expectations of the group manager and the mission statement of the group. Links to the Rules Page are located in the top right of the group pages.

Maintaining The Discussion

Since the group discussion wall gets crowded, only a short snippet of each conversation is shown. Click on the title of any discussion to be taken to a page that contains the entire discussion thread. Underneath the thread, you will find several options for participating:

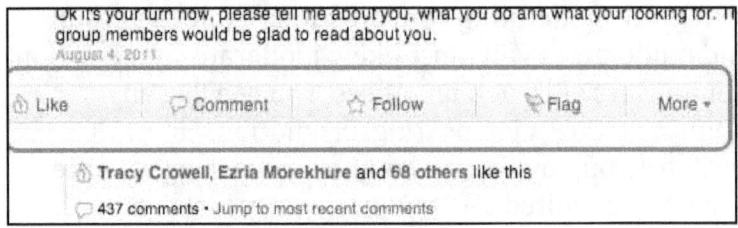

You can elect to: "Like" the discussion, reply with a comment, follow the discussion, flag it, and more.

Liking The Conversation

By liking, your name and picture will be added as a member who liked the conversation. This increases the visibility of the discussion, giving it a greater chance at being included in digest emails.

Comment

You can also add a comment of your own to the discussion. You can add your thoughts on the subject, respond with a question, and even include links to your own website, twitter account, etc. There's a small checkbox before posting your comment that asks you if you would like to receive an email notifications after new comments are added. Uncheck this option or else your inbox will get flooded. However, if the thread is very pertinent to your business, job search, or includes valuable information you wish to recall later, it may make sense to leave it checked.

Follow
The next option is to follow the conversation. By following a conversation, you will receive a notification whenever a new comment is made. This allows you to stay notified of new updates without having to venture back to the discussion or even participate. Be selective on which conversations you decide to follow.

Flagging The Conversation
This option is for moderating conversation. While the group owner and moderators will most likely moderate conversation, flagging empowers all group members. You can flag any conversation as either a job posting, promotion, or inappropriate. Group owners will either move flagged content to where it's better suited for group members, or remove the post after a certain amount of inappropriate flags.

More Tab
This last tab provides the option to reply privately to the conversation. This will allow you to reply to the person who started the dialogue via a private message. This is a great for directly addressing a person whose conversation struck a cord with you.

Networking With Group Members
Starting and joining discussions will eventually prompt the connecting with other group members; there are various ways to do that. You can of course send/receive an invitation and directly connect with members as 1st degree connections. You can also freely message other group members instead of connecting.

However, there are other ways to get on the radar of fellow group members.

You can "Follow" other group members, by clicking the "Follow *Their Name*" button under the thumbnail picture of the member's profile. This will make it so any of their group activity will show up in your home feed. When you come across group members whose input is extremely valuable, follow them so their content is fed into your home feed. This is 100x easier than digging through group discussions to find their contributions.

This is a great way for following the "thought leaders" of your groups. You will be able to comment and reply to their conversations directly from your home feed, allowing you to be one of the first to enter a follow up comment. This can help you get on their radar and initiate further communication.

Note: LinkedIn makes it so that you automatically "follow" your 1st Degree connections group contributions if there are groups that you are both members of.

Pro-Tip: You can see who the most influential members of your groups are by locating the "Top Influencers This Week" box in the right sidebar of the group page, below the group statistics box.

Jobs & Job Discussions

Starting, joining, and enhancing discussions within groups is by far the most rewarding aspect of group networking. This will lead to 1st degree connections, messages, and all sorts of professional opportunities and even friendships.

Another prominent advantage of joining groups is the ability to access the Jobs and Job Discussion sections. Depending on the group's settings, these sections may be left out.

Jobs

The listings found in the Jobs section are paid listings. LinkedIn has received compensations for these jobs to be posted to the main LinkedIn job board. Group managers and members can pinpoint opportunities from the job board and share them to the Group's Job section.

Since companies are paying big bucks for these postings, chances are these positions boast great opportunity. There's less of a chance that applications to these positions are disappearing into the black hole of HR. Click the title of any job listing and you will be taken to the original job posting found in the main Jobs area of LinkedIn. You can read through the full job listing, and then depending on the company's listing, you can apply directly on LinkedIn or will be provided a link taking you to the company's website where you can apply.

Jobs Discussion

This area contains jobs as well, but these are job postings that were posted for free. Be weary of the opportunities listed in the job discussions section. Since it costs nothing to post in this section, any group member can add a "job" here. Many times you will find pyramid scheme type opportunities lurking in this job sections area. However, don't completely ignore this section as many startup positions and lesser-known opportunities can be found hiding here.

Pro-Tip: Sort Your Jobs Starting With Newest
The Jobs tab by default lists all jobs by relevancy/popularity. To see the newest jobs postings, use the "sort by" button to show you listings by date posted. This will return newly posted jobs, giving you a chance to be one of the first to apply.

Sharing A Job
If the group manager allows all members to freely add jobs, there are 3 ways to post a job:

1. Posting a Job – This is the process of using a paid job listing to post in the Job section. These are not cheap, and currently cost around $300.

2. Search and Share – This is where we can instantly provide value to the group. Navigating to the jobs area of LinkedIn (the Jobs tab found in the main navigation menu), you can find newly posted jobs. First, search for jobs relevant to your group and then head to any of these relevant job listings. For each job posting, you will find a "Share" button underneath the apply button. This will allow you to share these opportunities to the Jobs section of any of your groups permitting this. Your group manager and fellow members will greatly appreciate your effort in populating the group's job board, especially if this leads to a group member landing a new position.

3. Post a Job Discussion – You can add job listings/postings found on websites other than LinkedIn, and even add your own offerings. Since these aren't formal LinkedIn job postings, make sure to add the contact details or provide a link to the opportunity if it's on another website. Again, these must be placed in the Jobs Discussion area, and not the Jobs area.

Optimizing Group Settings
Now that we've learned how to navigate our groups and interact with fellow members, we must adjust notification settings to keep us organized and sane. Since we will be joining several groups (up to 50 if you so desire), we must make sure

that our group settings are properly adjusted. We do not want to get bombarded by emails, spam, and overbearing group members.

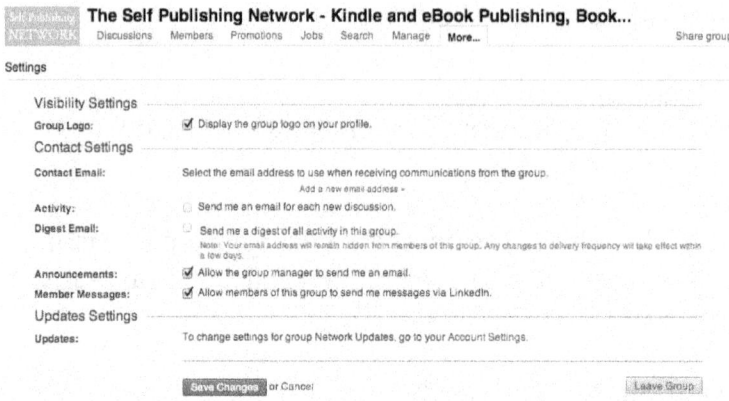

Locate the "More" tab in the navigation menu of your group. A dropdown will appear where you can click "Settings".

Settings Include:

Group Logo
Select whether or not you wish the group's logo/badge to appear in the group section of your profile. This should not matter, unless you've joined a group called "I hate my job and am looking for a new one" in which case you should uncheck the display button.

Contact Email
By default, LinkedIn will send email notifications to the email you've built your account with. You can change this email if you'd like to receive group emails to a different email account.

Activity
You can check this to receive an email notification of each new discussion added to the group. Uncheck this, unless you love getting bombarded with emails.

Digest Email

Here you can select to receive the roundup/digest emails. If you opt to receive emails, you will then be prompted to select whether you wish to receive these messages daily or weekly. These emails will contain a summary of discussion activity from the day or week. You may wish to receive weekly digests so that the best content comes is directed to your inbox. Weekly digests are also helpful in getting a feel for which type of conversations are popular within the group, and to see if any of your contributions made the cut.

Announcements

This controls whether the group manager can message you or not. This allows managers to send you a message at the most every 7 days. Depending on your group manager, these group messages can be very insightful as they usually have a pulse on what's happening in the industry and group. However, watch out for snake oil salesmen that started the group to get to your inbox. If that's the case, you will certainly want to opt out of these messages, or maybe even leave the group depending on the amount of value offered.

Member Messages

We've discussed this option throughout the book; this allows other members to freely message you, regardless of connection level. You should leave this option checked, as you want to provide a way for fellow members to contact you.

Updates

This links you to your account settings page. Here, you can select if and how the group's activity is shared to your home page. You will be shown and given control over the various updates that can be shown or left out.

Pro-Tips: Efficiently Manage Group Settings

Head to your main account settings page and navigate to the group communications tab. Here you will find group settings options in which you can control the settings of all of your groups at once. The most important option here is that you can set the frequency of group digest emails: daily, weekly, or never. However, you can't control the settings of group manager messages. For those messages, you will have to visit each group's settings page individually.

Make it a point to adjust your group's settings right after joining. After you join several groups, these email digests and group manager messages will begin piling up and you will have to circle back and make adjustments to each group's settings.

It's important to note how many messages and emails are distributed due to group activity. Since many people don't realize that these communications can be controlled from a settings page, many group discussions ends up in the personal inboxes of group members. You never know, but these group discussion digests may be appearing in the personal email inboxes of top executives and industry leaders. Make it a point to always contribute great content and discussion, as your participation and the value that you add will almost never go unnoticed, intentional or not.

The Bonus Chapters – Achieving Specific Goals On LinkedIn & Shortcuts That Will Get You There

Thus far, we've covered numerous networking strategies that will leave you more proficient than 95% of the users on LinkedIn. However, there are a few more features that we've yet to discuss, or have yet to discuss in the context for which these features are made most useful.

These bonus chapters provide additional insight for those with specific aims, such as those seeking jobs or looking for new client leads. Most of these insights will provide simple guidance, as entire books, courses, and trainings have been created for many of these specific situations (job searching, direct sales, recruiting).

We will focus strongly on leveraging the networking aspects we've already discussed, and include strategies or resources that you may wish to explore further on your own.

Lastly, we will look at a bunch of neat shortcuts you should enlist so that LinkedIn is carrying out networking tasks for you.

For Job Seekers & Career Changers

As the workplace continuously evolves, so does the job search and application process. The days of job postings in the newspaper linger on, but there are much more efficient ways to find new opportunities. While the process of job searching has evolved, networking still remains the most powerful catalyst for of attaining employment.

LinkedIn is a great tool for job searching, but an even better tool for networking. The best career opportunities are usually not achieved by replying to a job posting. Just because there is an available job in your area, doesn't mean that it's perfect for you. Your perfect job may be with a company that currently isn't hiring or requires certain skillsets you've yet acquired.

You may be a few years worth of experience away from your dream job, but that doesn't mean you should sit and wait until then. The last chapter on networking provides the key ingredients for building a valuable network; successful implementation of these key ingredients will return benefits well past the immediate future. For the more passive job seeker, or someone currently content in his or her line of work, building a rewarding network should be of the utmost priority.

However, many people these days are constantly seeking new career direction and opportunity. Many people are continuously applying to new jobs, switching companies, and heading down new career paths in reaction to the volatile employment landscape. If you are an active job seeker, LinkedIn offers several features that will enhance your job search of which we are about to cover. Additionally, there are a few networking strategies specific to the job search, not mentioned in the last chapter, which we will look at.

Finding The Best Job Postings

The most obvious feature that we've yet to discuss is the Job Board. Monster.com, CareerBuilder.com, and Indeed.com are quite helpful when job searching, but the LinkedIn Job Board is leaps and bounds more useful. While the same job postings may be found across all of these job boards, LinkedIn is the only website that integrates your professional network into the job application process. Let's discuss!

Searching For Jobs

Locate and click the Jobs tab located in your main navigation menu. You will be taken to the Job Board where you can search for jobs based on any criteria. Enter in keywords pertinent to the job you seek or keywords that represent your current skillsets into the search bar.

After you've entered your search criteria, LinkedIn will return a bunch of current postings them deem relevant. Now, we must filter through these results to find the best positions to apply to. In the left sidebar, the jobs filter will be selected already. Click the "Advanced" link for advanced search filters and search fields to appear. This best tactic is to narrow down results to only display job postings in which our connections are somehow connected to the posting.

Select the 1st and 2nd degree connections and refresh your search results. This will narrow down results that speak more to you and your network. The job postings that are returned will be with companies where a connection works, has worked, or is connected to someone that works there.

Why apply to jobs where you have no "in", when you have full control over which companies and positions you apply to!

There are tons of other filters to apply, the most important being location, the date the jobs were posted, and the company. These will help you narrow your results even further.

Applying To Jobs
Once you find a job listing that you wish to apply to, don't apply just yet!

On the job listing's page, there are two sections worth checking out first. First, in the sidebar you will be shown the profile of the person who posted the job. This is incredibly empowering, removing the anonymity and impersonal experience most feel when applying to jobs.

After applying to the job, you can message or InMail this person. Let them know of your application and your interest in the position. Although this may seem overbearing, most recruiters will make note of such effort and more often than not, your application will be at the top of their pile. At the very least, they will be exposed to your name in several places, which will incite a sense of connectivity.

Secondly, you should see if and you we are connected to the company as a whole. Any of your connections (of any degree) will be listed in the right sidebar if they are tied to this company. This gives you a few people to reach out to for help and/or an employee referral.

Employee referrals are highly respected, and most companies compensate their employees if their referrals turn into hires. Don't be afraid to ask for help. Even if you aren't too close with this connection, there may be an additional incentive for them passing on your application. Regardless, our connections should always be willing to help since we continuously provide value to our network.

Pro-Tip: Help Your Referral

In your outreach for referral request, tell your connections of the person that posted the job. This will save them time and help them quickly get your application/resume to the right person. They may even know this person on a personal basis, which will surely help your chances at landing an interview.

Applying For The Job
With a better grasp on the job posting and how it coincides with our network, we can now apply. LinkedIn allows those posting the job to collect applications directly on LinkedIn. If that's the case, when we hit the apply button, a pop up application box will be shown. LinkedIn will auto populate the application with our information and allow attachment of additional documents (cover letter, recommendations, etc.).

If the job poster rather not collect applications on LinkedIn, the Apply button will link us to the company's career website. Here, we will be asked us to apply within their career application and tracking system.

Set Your Job Search On Autopilot

Since the majority of our time should be spent networking, we can't waste time constantly combing through job postings. Taking advantage of LinkedIn's "Saved Searches" is highly recommended. This allows us to save job search criteria for future use. Not only that, we can tell LinkedIn to email us every day, week, or month when new jobs are posted that meet this criteria.

Once we've found keyword searches that yield an abundance of relevant opportunities, we will want to save these searches. At the top of the search results page there is a small green + icon next to the word "Save". Clicking on this button will prompt a pop up where we can name this newly saved search for future use. Additionally, we can select a frequency for which we will receive notifications of new jobs that match our search criteria.

There is no limit on the amount of saved searches that can be entered. Our entire job search can be set on autopilot, leaving us more time for higher value networking activities.

Following Companies

In addition to the Job Board and using Saved Searches, you can "follow" companies that have set up a company page. You can follow up to 1,000 companies if you so desire. By following a company, you will receive their updates in your home feed. Additionally, you can view updates of all the companies you follow by going to the "Companies" located underneath the Interests tab in the main navigation menu.

While not directly fruitful in terms of finding and applying to jobs, following companies is a great way to find those companies you are very interested in working for and getting to know what they are about. Company updates will sometimes include job opportunities, as they want to ensure their followers are first them in hearing about their openings. Additionally, if a recruiter or interviewer sees that you are already following their company, this certainly won't hurt your chances at landing the position.

Lastly, when searching for companies to follow using the search bar and advanced search filters, LinkedIn informs us of how many current job postings each company has, right next to their description. To find these positions, simply head to the company's page and visit the "Careers" tab. This is the best way for getting the most current job postings from companies of interest without even "following" them. Simply bookmark this "Careers" tab and stop in once a week. Alternatively, we can use the saved search feature to create company specific searches; this will result in new job opportunities being sent right to our inbox.

Additional Job Search Tips

Turn Your LinkedIn Profile Into A Resume

When going in for an interview and in need of a physical resume – LinkedIn can convert our profiles into a resume for us. There is an option to "Export to PDF" as listed as a dropdown option underneath the "Edit profile" button in our profile header. A PDF version of our resume will be instantly downloaded and ready for print or to be sent as an attachment.

To customize a resume, we can use LinkedIn's resume builder for picking out a custom template and making edits before converting to PDF.

Resume builder - http://resume.LinkedInlabs.com/

Search For Alumni
LinkedIn features a section dedicated solely to alumni connections. Listed under the network tab, there's a "Find Alumni" tab. Pulling from the school(s) listed on our profiles, LinkedIn provides a searchable list of alumni to connect with. We can narrow down the results with several filters including the specific school or university if we've attended more than one, the years in which the alumni attended, and the industry and location in which they work.

After we've narrowed down our job search to just a few companies and opportunities, identifying alumni in a position to help is highly suggested.

Seek Out Company Recruiters
One of the best ways for staying connected with companies of interest is to directly connect with the recruiters and HR professionals within the company.

Recruiters either work for a recruiting agency, where they work with several companies to find candidates, or they work

142

directly for one company. Even if there isn't a position currently available, a good recruiter will certainly connect with you and your name will be top of mind for any upcoming positions either with the company they work for, or for any of the companies their agency works for. Furthermore, many recruiters will want to engage in a short phone screening with you. This allows them the change to get to know you and determine what positions you may be a good fit for. Take the time to engage in these short phone screenings as recruiters may have opportunities that aren't posted online.

There are two ways to find the recruiters and HR representatives in charge of hiring. We've already looked at the first way, which is by looking through the persons who've posted the jobs found in the LinkedIn Job Board. Each job posting will list the person in charge of the job posting, and you will be able to connect, message, or InMail this person. Almost 100% of the time, these persons will have their settings to allow invitations to connect from any LinkedIn members as they greatly benefit from building a vast network.

The second way to find those responsible for recruiting matters is through search. Using the filters to only display "People" results, you can enter in the keywords that describe your desired position. Use the additional filters to narrow results by company, location, and other criteria that you are aware of.

As for the keywords to use, we will use what is referred to as a search string. For example, if we're looking for a marketing job at IBM, we should use this search string: "Recruiter" AND "Marketing".

We could then play around and try variations of this search string, as some companies don't title actually title recruiters as such.

You can try: "HR" AND "marketing" or "recruitment specialist" AND "marketing".

Using AND, OR, and other search operators in our search strings helps return highly targeted results. In the example above, by using the operator "AND", only profiles that contain the both terms, recruiter and marketing, will be returned.

There are tons of available search operators and best practices for how to use them, however, LinkedIn has so many advanced search filters built in that you really don't need to become a search operator expert.

You can visit this website to learn more about using search operators to fine tune your searches within LinkedIn. These search operators can be used within other search engines, such as Google, as well:
http://career-advice.monster.com/job-search/getting-started/boolean-basics-job-search/article.aspx

Pro-Tip: Learn The Lingo
With bigger companies, recruiters may be assigned to certain business lines and departments. Each company title's their departments and positions differently, so this is something you should take note of by visiting the company website or by searching employee titles on LinkedIn. Once you have the terminology for how these different business lines and positions are titled, you will be able to run highly targeted searches to find those in the most relevant position to help you.

For Sales Professionals, Business Development Professionals & Brand Ambassadors

On the other side of the LinkedIn networking spectrum, many users have aims of promoting their company's products/services. Whether you are a freelancer, a salesperson for a Fortune 500 company, or a branding professional, LinkedIn is the ideal platform for connecting with a targeted, affluent membership base.

No other social network boasts such a highly concentrated platform of professionals. LinkedIn themselves state that their membership 'is the most affluent, influential, and educated audience on the social web".

Many users are in a position where they have purchasing power on behalf of their company or run their own company.

LinkedIn is hands down the best platform for marketing B2B services and solutions. Not only can LinkedIn be used as a thriving lead and sales generator, but market research can also be conducted by learning about the problems and opportunity gaps within various industries. Utilizing group discussions and direct outreach, opportunity for potential products and services will present itself.

Referencing the previous chapter, proper networking strategy and etiquette provides most of the strategy necessary in delivering results, especially messaging and group discussion strategy. However, let's explore several other features that may be useful for those looking to improve their business via LinkedIn.

Creating A Company Page

For those looking to formally own some company real estate on LinkedIn, one can create a company page. Just because the Fortune 500 companies have a LinkedIn Company Page, should you?

Most certainly!

The advantages of creating a company page outweigh not creating one, and it doesn't require much effort to maintain one. While it shouldn't take precedence over the earlier discussed networking strategies, building a company page is a great way for validating your company's presence on LinkedIn. Interested persons and businesses can visit this page to learn more about your company. Job seekers can see your current job openings and businesses can learn about your products and services.

It's important to understand the difference between a company page and a group. A company page is made specifically for companies looking to claim their presence on LinkedIn. It acts as an informative resource, providing visitors a place to learn about the company; someone from the company manages it.

LinkedIn Groups are designed specifically for members of LinkedIn. Groups provide a centralized discussion point for members to interact; any LinkedIn member can manage a group.

Company pages can only be followed, whereas groups can be joined. This explains why groups are more useful, as they allow for interaction and combined members' contributions make them a valuable resource. Company pages involve less interaction, allowing companies to get their updates and information out to those interested in them. For those familiar with the difference between Facebook Pages and Facebook Groups, this is the same thing.

So why make not just make a group? Great question. Groups are reserved for creating a community around a central topic, industry, profession, or aim/goal. You will occasionally come across what you think are branded groups, but these are usually alumni groups or organizations unrelated to the company, such as the Coca Cola Alumni Networking Group. Nobody will be pitching any of Coca Cola's products in this group. Members instead will be networking with other former employees to find new career opportunities.

Creating a group is still a feasible option as long as the group is concentrated around a specific topic or profession. For example, a graphic designer could start a group called – Graphic & Web Design Professionals. Running groups are much more work intensive and we will discuss creating a group in the next section.

Building Your Page
LinkedIn members do find value in company pages. Visitors to your company page will be able to find company related news and updates, job listings, and current products/services.

Additionally, a company page allows current employees to list that they work for your company in their profile, and this mention will link to the company page. Other LinkedIn members can now search for employees of your company using the company filter, provided in advanced search, to learn more about a desired position by contacting current employees. This transparency and career openness is greatly appreciated by today's workforce.

There aren't many requirements for starting a company page, other than that an existing company page cannot exist, and a company email address is required to initiate the process. That means the person creating the company page must have a company email, so john@cocacola.com and not john@gmail.com.

Company pages are constantly evolving – any instruction or content placed in this book would most likely be outdated in a few months. Because creating a company page is a less common undertaking, and not as valuable as group creation – here are a few resources to help in creating and maintaining your company page.

LinkedIn FAQ - http://help.LinkedIn.com/app/answers/detail/a_id/1561
Creating a Group Walkthrough - http://socialmediatoday.com/node/1255091

Creating Your Own LinkedIn Group

To be blunt, creating a group with hundreds and thousands of contributing members is a very tall task. However, creating a successful group is by far the most rewarding effort one can undertake when building their network or business on LinkedIn.

The hardest part of managing a group is gaining initial traction. You must have a large network, or be connected with those that can help promote the group. It takes months to build initial traction. Once there are several hundred members, the group will begin to naturally acquire new members.

This happens for several reasons. Assuming you have created a relevant group and have properly titled/described the group, the group will begin to appear in the group search results for your desired keywords. Additionally, connections of group members will start to take notice of the groups their connections are part of, with your group's logo plastered to all of the members' profiles. There's even the chance that members will join your group in order to take advantage of the unrestricted messaging of other group members.

Taking this all into consideration, you are probably wondering if it is worth it to create a group. Let's take a look at all of the benefits of creating a group and then you can decide if the work is worth the reward:

Messaging Capabilities

LinkedIn used to provide group owners with access to members' emails, but recently removed this capability. However, group owners still can initiate direct conversation with group members, essentially giving group owners their own email messaging system at no cost.

Weekly Messages To Members

You are allowed to send members a message every 7 days and these will end up in your members' inboxes, respective of their group settings.

Auto-Response Welcome Message
When members join your group, you can have a welcome message automatically sent to them. You can tailor this message to speak to what the group is about, how they should participate, and even direct them to your own newsletter or website outside of LinkedIn.

Manager's Choice
Owners can decide to highlight a discussion thread, labeled manager's choice, which is positioned in the top right corner of the group homepage. This is a great way for directing visitors to a certain discussion. Good use of the manager's choice includes a welcome thread where members can introduce themselves. People love talking about themselves, and this gets everyone involved with the group right from the start.

Generating Leads & Driving Traffic To Your Website
Boosting your website's traffic can of course lead to more customers. You can use the various messaging capabilities to send relevant content from your website to your members. Also, there are several other places, including the group profile, where you can add your website's link.

Ultimately, you'll want to reap rewards of creating a thriving group in the form of sales of your products/services. By creating a group where valuable discussion is the norm, incredible content is shared, and members find career opportunities, you will be in a powerful position.

You won't have to work hard to sell your products/services; members will always be reminded, through messaging and group discussion, that you are the go to person on your group's topic. Once the group begins to grow organically, you will have a lead generation machine working for you.

Creating The Group

Groups can be created in minutes, and aren't restricted by any rules as to who can create a group. Again, groups are constantly evolving and listing out the steps would be frivolous.

Here is a great resource for setting up a group - http://learn.LinkedIn.com/group-management/

However, there are best practices for creating groups that must be discussed in order for your group to achieve success. Let's examine how to optimize your group.

Optimizing Your Group

Proper Title, Description, and Logo
You need to make sure all of your group's information isn't conflicting with any trademarks, brands, or existing companies. This should be easy to avoid because you will want to title your group based on keywords that will both inform people as to what your group is about and also be searched for by users. "Front End Programmers Network - HTML, CSS, and JavaScript Coders" is a great title because it doesn't include any brands or companies, and users know that this group is specifically for front-end programmers.

This paints a picture as to what group discussions will be about. Using this same type of approach, you will build out your group description to include a longer pitch as to why users should join the group. Include industry specific keywords, as this will help your group appear in relevant searches.

Lastly, make a logo for your group that is very easy to read. Forget using images or clipart; just use a very readable font to spell out the group name so people can tell by the thumbnail image what the group is. Ideal logo images are currently sized at 100 pixels x 50 pixels in a JPEG, GIF, and PNG format.

Use of Sub Groups
If you are creating a group based around a large topic such as "Web Design", you can utilize the sub group feature to help built out smaller, more target groups. Examples of subgroups would include "Front End Web Designers", "Back End Programmers" or even a geo-targeted group "New York City Web Design".

This provides those with a large undertaking, such as being in charge of nationwide sales, a way to initiate more targeted discussions with more group members. Any member that joins a subgroup will automatically become members of the parent group. This is a great way to build the membership of the original group, all while providing value at a more targeted level. Messages sent to members of the main group can also be sent to members of the subgroup in one click, so communication doesn't have to be fragmented.

Gaining Influential Members

The best way to get your group off the ground is through the support of your network, and through influential members in your space. By getting influential persons to join your group, their connections will see an update about them joining in their home feed. Additionally, members looking to interact with this member will now have an environment to do so, by joining your group.

Pro-Tip: Collaborate With Group Managers

Don't have the time or resources to start your own group? You can always become group manager of an already successfully established group. If you know someone who runs a successful group or are member of a group where the owner finds yours contributions valuable, you may look to collaborate with this person. They can promote you to a manager position, where you will have the power to send out messages and interact directly with the members. This is the shortcut alternative to creating your own group, and you will still reap the rewards of a large, targeted membership.

Additional Features & How To Utilize Them

There are some features that we've left out because they are not essential to properly networking on Linkedin. We've including them here as a reference as many readers may be able to extract value from these features.

LinkedIn Today

LinkedIn Today features news and insights from around LinkedIn, displaying the most discussed and shared content. You can customize the news you see in your LinkedIn Today's news feed by following certain Channels and Influencers.

Channels

LinkedIn curates channels and there are currently 23 different channels that you can follow. These channels are broad in scope, such as "Technology" and "Your Career", and help filter contributed content from the most influential people and news sources as related to the channel topic.

Influencers

You can also choose to follow Influencers. These are thought leaders, CEOs, and innovators within their respective market and industry. Influencers are chosen by LinkedIn and are selected through an application process. This is a great way for getting more insightful and personalized commentary about what's happening in your industry.

Once you've selected some Channels and Influencers to follow, you can view the newest posts from the LinkedIn Today page. You can view all content at once, or break it down by influencers and channels. You can access the LinkedIn Today homepage at: http://www.linkedin.com/today/ or by visiting the "Influencers" tab found in the dropdown of the Interest Tab located in your main navigation menu.

Pro Tip – Getting Your Content Featured

If your content, in the form of blog posts, whitepapers, and media, is gaining a lot of attention naturally – you can apply to have it featured on LinkedIn Today. Send an email to LinkedIn's business development team at publisher@LinkedIn.com and notify them of your content's current success and how it would benefit readers of a certain Channel.

OpenLink Network

We've yet to discuss the OpenLink Network. This is because it is currently made available to premium subscribers only.

If you are a premium subscriber, the OpenLink network allows any member of LinkedIn to message you for free, regardless of whether they are in your network or not. You will have the option to turn OpenLink on/off and an icon will appear next to your name on your profile and in search results. Once opted in, anyone can now reach out to you without having to use an Introduction or InMail.

According to LinkedIn statistics, OpenLink members receive 7 times more messages per month than other users. OpenLink members also gain access to an advanced search filter, which targets other OpenLink members. Remember, this feature is only optional for those with a premium subscription.

Pro-Tip – Messaging OpenLink Members

You don't have to have a premium subscription to take advantage of OpenLink. Although basic members can't opt-in to the OpenLink Network, they can freely message OpenLink members. Look to see if there is an OpenLink icon next to those members you wish to message; if they are part of the network, you can message them by selecting "Send InMail". The one caveat is that you have an Introduction available. You won't be charged an Introduction for sending this OpenLink message, nor will you be charged an InMail. It will simply redirect to OpenLink message page where you can freely message this user.

LinkedIn Ads

If you are looking to generate leads, increase sales, and have a budget – advertising may be perfect for you. The key to remember is that LinkedIn is ideal for conducting B2B campaigns and NOT B2C type campaigns.

We are again working with the "professional network" and purchases stem from professional decision makers. Not many users on LinkedIn are looking to whip out their wallets/purses to purchase a consumer product, and even if they are, the margins are not justifiable for low priced consumer products.

LinkedIn's very affluent membership includes small business owners, employees in position to manage their company's budget and spending decisions, and powerful company executives looking for companywide software solutions to increase their business's profitability.

Knowing this distinction between B2B and B2c is crucial, and this should help you determine if LinkedIn ads may benefit you or your company. To get started, here's an overview of the advertising program:

http://partner.LinkedIn.com/ads/info/Ads_faqs_updated_en_US.html?utm_source=li&utm_medium=el&utm_campaign=gate-c

Additional Resources

Resume Builder
You can now transform your profile into a resume within minutes. Choose your template, edit the content, and then save as a PDF. Additionally, you will get a link to your resume's own webpage, which you can share across your social networks and even in your email signature.

http://resume.LinkedInlabs.com/

Mobile - LinkedIn App
One of the better business apps around, you can quickly access all of the same features and content found on the website. It's a must have app for those on the go and it's a great supplement for recalling contact information of your connections when out and about.

Apple Store - https://itunes.apple.com/us/app/LinkedIn/id288429040?mt=8
Google Play Store - https://play.google.com/store/apps/details?id=com.LinkedIn.android&hl=en
Blackberry - http://appworld.blackberry.com/webstore/content/7605/?countrycode=US
Windows - http://www.windowsphone.com/en-us/store/app/LinkedIn/bdc7ae24-9051-474c-a89a-2b18f58d1317

Email – Microsoft Outlook Toolbar
For those using Microsoft Outlook for their email client, you can use this toolbar to integrate your LinkedIn with your address book. Supercharge your network by putting a face to all of your contacts, and discover new contacts when others are included in emails conversations.

https://www.LinkedIn.com/static?key=outlook_toolbar_downl
oad

Website – Share Your profile

For those with their own website, portfolio, or blog – insert one of these LinkedIn badges to bring visitors to your public profile. Just copy and paste any of these badges right into your website.

https://www.LinkedIn.com/profile/profile-badges

LinkedIn Training – LinkedIn University

LinkedIn continues to build out their library of helpful resources and training videos to help users become more proficient on their platform.

http://university.LinkedIn.com/career-services/

Before You Go...

Did you find this book helpful? Was it worth the few dollars?

Were you able to learn and apply these strategies in helping catapult your career?

Whether you loved it, found it useless, or are somewhere in between, your opinion is valued highly by us, the Amazon Marketplace, and most importantly – **fellow readers**.

Please visit the book's listing on Amazon to leave a review!

With future updates provided to you for no additional cost, all feedback helps improve each new edition.

That will help inform future readers about what the book entails, and allows us to make critical adjustments in future editions – it only takes less than a minute.

Thank You,

Brian & Jonathan

www.ingramcontent.com/pod-product-compliance
Lightning Source LLC
Chambersburg PA
CBHW051806170526
45167CB00005B/1904